THE FISHING
HANDBOOK

THE FISHING
HANDBOOK

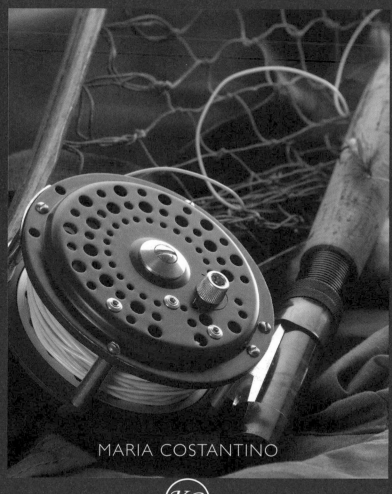

MARIA COSTANTINO

KB

© 2010 Kerswell Farm Ltd

This edition published by King Books

Printed 2012

This book is distributed in the UK by
Parkham Books Ltd
Barns Farm, Boraston
Tenbury Wells
Worcestershire
WR15 8NB

enquiries@dsbg.co.uk

ISBN: 978-1-906239-50-3

DS0176. The Fishing Handbook

Creative Director: Sarah King
Editor: Anna Southgate
Project Editor: Sally MacEachern
Designer: Jade Sienkiewicz

Printed in Singapore

3 5 7 9 10 8 6 4 2

CONTENTS

COARSE FISHING

"Of all nacyons and countres England is beeste seryed of Fysshe- not onely al manre of see fysshe but also of freshe water fysshe- an al manre of salte fysshe."

The Fyrst Boke of the Introduction of Knowledge (1542) by Andrew Boorde

Writing in the middle of the 16th century, Boorde was clearly extolling the virtues of his homeland in an age that saw many voyages of discovery as nations competed with each other for territories and colonies overseas. Today, we have knowledge of a huge range of fish species and aquatic environments beyond our shores, and are aware that what constitutes modern angling for sport or pleasure will change from place to place.

Whatever their language or nationality, there are some things that unite fishermen- and women: first there is the passion for fishing with a rod, line and a hook whether for sport or pleasure. Second, is the sense of being close to nature. Indeed anglers worldwide have been active in maintaining and restoring rivers, lakes and seas to maintain and support biodiversity. Fishing seasons are strictly enforced and 'catch and return' policies ensure that fish stocks are kept at optimum levels to ensure a healthy future for both the fish and the angler.

Water makes up 70% of our planet's surface but the underwater realm largely remains a mystery. What is sometimes described as 'fishing luck' in fact depends on the angler's knowledge and understanding of the species and habits of the fish that is being targeted and the environment in which that species lives. Across the world, anglers are constantly devising new artificial baits and tying new fly patterns; manufacturers are developing new materials for rods and lines, and the growing popularity of fishing from boats that has allowed anglers to reach new fishing grounds. With these developments, new methods of fishing have evolved as 'new' species of fish have caught the angler's attention. While this means that angling knowledge and skills are always changing, one thing remains constant and that is the angler's willingness to share advice, hints and tips with newcomers- and stories of 'the one that got away'.

INTRODUCTION

Whether you are novice angler who has been 'hooked' on fishing and want to improve your skills, an experienced angler whose aim is to catch the perfect specimen fish, or a complete beginner who will be enjoying the peace and tranquillity of a day's fishing regardless of whether any fish are actually caught, The Handbook of Fishing introduces the three main modern angling disciplines of coarse fishing, fly fishing and sea fishing. It offers information on the different tackles and baits, on choosing locations and watercraft, as well as identifying different species of fish.

WATERCRAFT

Experienced anglers are successful anglers because they have learnt watercraft. Watercraft is not just about targeting likely fishing 'hot spots' or 'good swims' along rivers, it also takes account of when – and when not – to fish, the speed of the current, the clarity of the water, wind direction and the landscape under the water's surface.

RIVER CONDITIONS

A good river swim depends on the species of fish the angler is targeting: big fish don't like to battle against strong currents for long periods. Instead they prefer to conserve their strength for the stretches of river with a more even flow. Big fish also prefer to stay close to the bottom of the river, where the slower waters they prefer meet the faster waters that deposit food. From this deeper position, the bigger fish can snatch food from the upper, faster, current as the food passes. The presence of such areas of water on rivers is usually indicated by what's called a 'crease', where the river surface is disturbed by the convergence of faster and slower bodies of water. The inside curve of a river bend is a good place to look for a crease.

ABOVE FISHING IN SPARKLING WATERS.

RIGHT EACH RIVER HAS ITS OWN CHARACTER.

LEFT THE RUSHING WATER OF A STREAM

In cold weather and in winter, fish like to gather in the deeper pools and holes in the riverbed, which offer better protection from rapid changes in water temperature. Conversely, in warm weather and in summer, the fish are likely to be more widely dispersed throughout the river. Because fish like well-oxygenated water, rivers with weir pools can be particularly good fishing spots in summer months.

Crystal-clear rivers mean that anglers can see the fish, but the fish can also see the angler. Angling in such waters requires a stealthy and quiet approach: experienced anglers look for 'pegs' (convenient fishing areas) with cover on the far bank side – perhaps with bushes or tree branches that drape over and into the river. Undercut riverbanks and rafts of debris, such as small tree branches and twigs that have got snagged by the river bank, are good places to concentrate on, especially if you want to hook a chub.

Heavy rain raises river levels and water run-off from the surrounding land can lead to flood. Expert anglers watch the rivers at this time looking for 'colour' – a fine mud that has been deposited into the river. This colour gives fish cover and they become adventurous about leaving the undercut banks and rafts in daylight. Because the river is swollen and faster flowing, the fish have to expend more energy than they would just idling away in clear water, so they will be hungry and need to feed frequently. Experienced anglers wait for the flow to subside so that the colour begins to drop out of the water and they can see just under the surface: they also know that the hungry fish cannot see very far so they'll use large, highly visible, smelly bait to tempt them.

RIGHT THE CLEAR WATERS OF A CHALK STREAM.

ABOVE EACH RIVER IS UNIQUE.

RIVER TYPES

There is an extremely wide variety of river types, each with its own distinctive character: some rivers flow through varied landscapes, which lead to several zones within a river system. The make up of the land that the river flows through determines the nature of the environment, which in turn determines the species that live within it.

ABOVE FLY-FISHING FOR BROWN TROUT.

ABOVE SMALL BROWN TROUT PROVIDE
EXCITING SPORT.

upper reaches

This section tends to be fast flowing, shallow and clear. Brown trout are abundant throughout this section and can provide exciting sport for the fly-fisherman during the spring and summer. In winter months
salmon travel high up into this region to what are termed 'redds' (gravel beds) to spawn. The salmon
are protected from anglers at this vulnerable time to safeguard future stocks. This area is typically moorland or mountain country and there is limited food for the fish; as a result the fish are often small. The
pH of the water is liable to be slightly acidic.

middle reaches

The brown trout are joined by grayling and a few coarse fish, such as dace, in the middle reaches, which are fast flowing and deeper in parts. Salmon are also to be found especially after spates or heavy downpours, which encourage them to forge upstream. Farmland and woodland dominate the landscape throughout this section. Food for the species within the river becomes more abundant and fish like trout are potentially bigger. However anglers find themselves competing with herons, kingfishers and otters.

ABOVE THE RIVER WYE MEANDERS THROUGH FARM AND WOODLAND.

ABOVE LEFT THE ESTUARY
CHANNELS AS SEEN FROM THE AIR.

ABOVE RIGHT THE TIDAL ZONE
HOLDS A WIDE RANGE OF FOOD
FOR BIRDS AND FISH.

lower reaches

Coarse fish dominate these wider and slower moving parts of a river. The water is slightly coloured most of the time. Bream, roach, chub, pike and carp can be caught to a good size down to the tidal limit and slightly beyond.

BELOW WATER LILIES IN A PERFECT TENCH SWIM.

CANALS

Canals are wonderful places for novice anglers to begin fishing: they are easily accessible, day-fishing permits are inexpensive, and there are plenty of small fish, such as roach, gudgeon and perch, to catch. There are plenty of challenges for the experienced angler, too, and some big fish – carp, chub and bream – to be caught. A good way to approach canal fishing is to think of a canal as a man-made river. Like a river, a canal has particular features, primarily a deep boat channel that runs down the centre of the watercourse, on either side of which are shallow ledges, and a towpath running alongside.

ABOVE LEFT REFLECTIONS
IN STILL WATERS.

ABOVE THIS BRIGHTLY COLOURED
GOLDEN ORFE CAME FROM A SMALL
STILL WATER.

ABOVE RIGHT A TREE-SHROUDED
LAKE.

With the exception of eels, most fish in a canal prefer the waters above the shallow ledges to the deep channel, where they have to battle against the turbulence created by passing boats. The younger, smaller (and more foolhardy) fish gather on the near side (the towpath) of the canal while wiser older fish make for the quieter shallows on the far side of the canal, well away from noise, people and predators. They also stay clear of any turbulence in the water, especially where nearby lock gates are opened and shut.

As in rivers, the smart fish stay among the features on the far bank such as reeds or overhanging bushes and branches. Experienced anglers know that they have to fish very close to these in order to get a bite. Casting with accuracy, using a waggler float (see page 60) or leger lead (see page 56) is very difficult in this kind of location, which is why anglers use long poles – some 14m (46ft)

long instead. With a very small amount of line between the tip of the long pole and the float, the serious canal angler can push his bait right up to the far bank without having to cast.

Even without a long pole, it is possible to fish with success on canals: pegs on either side of canal bridges – especially busy road bridges – are good spots because the construction and traffic deter cormorants, one of the angler's main competitors. An added bonus to the angler is that small fish are more likely to gather for safety near the bridges, as are pike because they follow the little fishes for their food. Other good pegs can be found around boat turning bays, where the construction of the canal provides a wide basin. These areas are protected from the tow created by the opening and closing of lock gates and can be home to large shoals of bream and tench.

STILL WATERS

A vast range of still water is available to the angler, including lakes – both natural and man-made – reservoirs, tiny ponds, meres, quarry and gravel pits. Each of these will have developed its own, complex ecosystem, which the wise angler should try to understand. Because there is no flow to carry the bait to the fish and draw them into your peg, the angler has to locate the fish. Start by looking at the wind direction: a fairly stiff prevailing breeze blows items of food across the water's surface to an area where it amasses and attracts fish. The experienced angler fishes into the wind in this situation.

The next thing the seasoned angler looks for on still water is a natural feature, such as an island, a mass of lily pads or a reed bed. This is because fish are attracted to any feature that provides them with shelter and protection. Look for pegs where you can cast to within 60–90cm (2–3ft) of an island, or where you can drop bait close to reeds or lilies. And don't overlook the waters at your feet: the temptation to cast straight out into open water is great but you may well find plenty of fish just 60cm (2ft) from the bank on which you are sitting.

In recent years there has been a huge upsurge in small, heavily stocked waters. These are ideal for the beginner or match angler. Fish are relatively easy to catch and provide almost guaranteed sport. The large volume of angler's bait introduced into these waters ensures good growth rates despite the often small quantities of natural food. Carp are the fish most often stocked, as they grow quickly, fight hard when hooked and are relatively hardy.

upland lakes, tarns, lochs and reservoirs

These waters are often slightly acidic and are similar, in some ways, to the upland river. Brown trout, rainbow trout and, in some cases, char can be found. Coarse fish are not generally abundant, although there may be a few predatory species such as pike and perch. In lakes and lochs that river systems flow through, migratory fish, such as salmon and sea trout, are caught. In these environments fish like pike can grow to a large size. Many reservoirs are heavily stocked with rainbow trout on a 'put and take' basis, in order to provide good sport for the fly-fisherman.

ABOVE LEFT ENJOYING THE
SOLITUDE.

ABOVE THE WILD EXPANSE OF AN
UPLAND LAKE.

ABOVE RIGHT GRAVEL PITS PROVIDE
ANGLERS WITH A WEALTH OF
OPPORTUNITY.

lowland lakes, reservoirs and meres

Many species of fish inhabit these waters, including coarse fish as well as trout stocked as above. The depth often determines the nature of these waters. Large shallow waters generally have more abundant weed growth and silt deposits, thus providing a rich habitat for water life to flourish. In ideal water a food chain develops that supports a vast range of fish. Reservoirs are often quite deep, as they are usually formed by damming a watercourse in a valley. Surrounding features give clues as to what lies beneath the surface – for example, a stream flowing into a reservoir often means a deeper channel. Steep banks generally mean deep water close in, while a gently sloping bank means shallow water close in.

gravel pits

While many commercial fisheries are completely flat and featureless below the surface – no submerged trees or branches, and often no great drop-offs in depth – gravel pits have deep craters and pits where gravel was excavated, as well as large ledges (where excavating vehicles moved around) and wide, shallow bars where waste materials were deposited.

Each pit therefore has a different 'landscape' and the angler needs to spend a little time exploring and mapping the pit to locate the features that at-

tract fish. The first step in mapping out a gravel pit is by a technique known as 'leading,' which is in essence plumbing depths all over the pit using a 28–57g (1–2oz) lead tied to the end of a line with a marker float above it. When the rig is cast out, the lead sinks to the bottom of the pit and the line is retrieved until the float is pulled down under the water and hits the lead. The line is then paid out a metre (or a foot) at a time until the float reappears on the surface. Counting the number of metres (or feet) of line released allows you to calculate the depth of the water at that point and helps you to chart the changes in depth as you cast in different areas. As you move from swim to swim, you can build up a picture – or indeed draw out a picture on graph paper – of the profile of the pit's bed and from this picture you can plan your assault on the fish.

As with river fish, those in gravel pits 'move around' according to the weather and temperature: in winter, the fish head for areas with the deepest waters, as these are the warmest and where the fish will be. In summer (and in warmer spells in winter), the sides of shallower ledges and bars are where the food is. And where there is food, there are fish. Gravel pits are also 'clear venues': you and the fish may be able to see each other, so night-time might be the best time to go fishing, or try overcast and breezy days, when the light under the water is less intense. When you do catch a worthy fish, it's a good idea too to make a note of the time, as the big fish in gravel pits have set feeding times that may only last for an hour or so each day.

For thousands of years, man has taken his food from nature by hunting, gathering and fishing. Early man probably caught fish with his bare hands and then gradually realised that sharp 'pins' and other primitive fishing equipment were quite effective. Archaeological finds show that after around 40,000 BC, three main types of fishing equipment were being used. Spears appear to have been used for fishing in shallow lakes and rivers as well as at sea; woven nets and traps were also placed in strategic locations, and — of interest to modern anglers — the hook appeared in use in southern Europe in around 30,000 BC. At that time, hooks were chiefly made from bone, although wood was probably also used to fashion barbed hooks. These hooks were attached to lines made of animal sinews, long hairs - such as horse hair - and even thin, tough plants, such as vines and grasses. By around 4,000 BC the art of angling had been refined: Egyptian tomb paintings depict scenes of fishing with rods, lines and hooks.

ABOVE A SELECTION OF TACKLE.

MODERN TACKLE

The years shortly after World War II saw the development of new, man-made materials and led to the development of glass-fibre rods and synthetic lines. Solid glass-fibre rods were soon replaced by hollow versions, making them lighter, stronger and more flexible. Today, the vast majority of coarse fishing rods are made from carbon fibre, a material that is unsurpassed for its combination of strength, rigidity and lightness, and you can buy rods from 1.8–6m (6–20ft) long.

A vast array of tackle is available for today's angler. To get started you do not need to spend huge sums of money: more important is an understanding of what is required of the tackle you intend to purchase, as each item is designed with a specific job in mind. Remember that the basic principles of angling are to present a bait or lure to a fish in order to tempt the fish onto the hook, and then bring the fish to the boat or bank to either release or eat. Consequently, the tackle you use needs to be capable of casting or placing the bait where the fish is located. It also needs to be strong enough to land the fish, yet not so apparent to the fish that it may decline the invitation to take the bait.

Tip Ring

Reel Seat

Butt Ring

ABOVE THE ANATOMY OF A ROD.

Butt

RODS

The butt of a rod is the thick end where the reel is attached. The rod's main body is tapered through to its tip. A series of line guides or rod rings are whipped to the rod; the size of these rings is determined by the type of reel, the line to be used and weight to be cast. There are some rods without rings, the line being threaded through the rod's hollow centre instead. Rods are tapered from butt to tip in varying degrees depending on the rod's purpose. The rod has what is termed as a 'test curve', which is the weight needed to compress the rod to an angle of 90º. The rod's action also varies from 'through action' to 'tip action' – terms that refer to the rod's flexibility from butt to tip.

ABOVE LEFT THE REEL IS ATTACHED TO THE ROD AT THE REEL SEAT USING VARIOUS TYPES OF FITTINGS.

LEFT ROD TIPS VARY GREATLY ACCORDING TO THEIR PURPOSE.
(TOP) A HEAVY DUTY BOAT ROD.
(MIDDLE) A SPINNING ROD.
(BOTTOM) A LIGHTWEIGHT TROUT FLY ROD.

These technical aspects are perhaps difficult to explain, but have great relevance in the way that a rod is intended to perform. To describe it in simpler terms, imagine flicking a rubber with a ruler and visualising the rubber flying across a schoolroom. Now imagine doing the same with a floppier piece of plastic. In angling, the line is attached to the 'flying object' that has to be retrieved – and may be very heavy if a fish has taken the bait. The rod now has to 'cushion' the strain on the line.

The purposes of the rod, reel, line and hook:

- The rod is used to propel the terminal tackle to its destination.
- The reel stores the line.
- The line connects angler to terminal tackle and bait.
- The hook holds the bait and then hopefully the fish.

While the tackle you choose needs to be carefully matched to the fishing environment and to the type of fish you want to catch, it must also be a pleasure to use, since this is the prime motivation for going fishing.

The rod is often described as an extension of the angler's arm and in many styles of angling the rod seems to be part of the body. Indeed the pleasure of propelling bait into the water is part of the joy of angling. The purpose of the rod is to cast, or place the terminal tackle and bait. The rod is also used to keep the line clear of obstructions when retrieving the bait or fish. Furthermore, the tip of the rod can also be used to detect when a fish takes the bait (referred to as 'a bite').

A rod is designed to meet the following criteria:

- To cast or place the bait.
- To absorb any stresses placed upon the line during casting.
- To absorb the stresses of hooking and landing fish.
- In some cases, to indicate a fish's bite at the tip of the rod.
- To transmit the sensation of a fish pulling at the end of the line to the angler.
- To give anglers pleasure in its use.

Just as there are numerous different fish to be caught, there are many types of rod with which to catch them. The rods used depend not only on the fish, but on the environment and those used in coarse fishing include poles; match or float rods; leger or quiver-tip rods; carp or pike rods; spinning or lure rods. There are also specialist fly-fishing, beach-casting and boat fishing rods.

poles

A pole is a rod that is used without a reel to place, or swing, bait into position. Poles are generally used in freshwater fishing to catch coarse fish from still water or slow-moving rivers and canals, but they are also widely used in competition fishing.

Basic poles were commonly used before the introduction of the reel, and poles made of cane were traditionally used for roach fishing on rivers such as the Thames. Although they went out of fashion for some time, they have made a big comeback since the introduction of modern rod-making materials that enable them to be extremely long (in excess of 13m/42ft 6in) and light in weight while remaining relatively rigid. A length of elastic is attached to the interior of the pole and connected to the line to act as a buffer and help prevent line breakage. Poles are often used in freshwater match fishing to present bait precisely, as well as to catch large numbers of fish very quickly.

Short poles, or whips, are often only a few metres long: these are ideal first rods for beginners or for children, as they are relatively cheap to buy and there are no reels to get tangled up with the line. Simply dangling a float with a bait suspended beneath it can yield a good number of small fish.

float or match rods

These rods tend to come in three sections of equal length: they can measure between 3.7 and 4.6m (12–15ft) long. Very light in weight, they are designed for float fishing using light tackle and are likely to have a test curve of between 340 and 560g (12oz–1lb 4oz). The lines used with these rods have a small diameter and a low breaking strain, typically 453g–2.7kg (1–6lb). The rod rings are arranged so that the line is kept clear of the rod – a line can cling to a wet rod and impede the trajectory of the float when the angler is casting a light weight.

Float rods are used to catch many different species of fish in many different environments: on rivers they are primarily used for catching roach, dace and grayling because the long rod gives excellent control of the tackle: it allows the float to drift or 'trot' downstream while, at the same time, allowing the line to be lifted

ABOVE POLES CAN PRESENT BAIT WITH GREAT
ACCURACY.

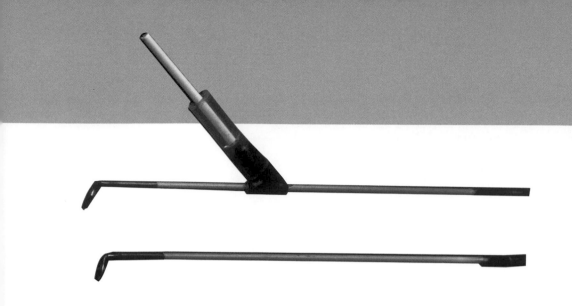

LEFT GAZING INTENTLY AT A PAIR OF QUIVER TIPS.

ABOVE THE TOP QUIVER TIP HAS AN ATTACHMENT FOR A BETA LIGHT, SO THAT THE TIP CAN BE SEEN IN THE DARK.

from the river current and run straight downstream. In still waters, the rod is used to target most coarse species. Rods for waggler fishing (see page 60), used on both still and running water, tend to have a hollow tip section and plenty of 'give' or flexibility below to allow the angler to make long, sweeping strikes at a distance. Rods for stick float fishing – where the angler has to make fast and repeated strikes at cautious fish like roach – tend to be quite stiff up to the top 60cm (2ft), with a soft tip 'spliced' in to absorb the shocks of fast strikes at short distances. In general though, a good quality, hollow-tipped 4m (13ft) float rod with a 'snappy action' is a good rod for the novice to start with.

leger or quiver-tip rods

Leger or quiver-tip rods are designed for fishing bait on the bottom. They are generally two-piece rods 2.7–3.7m (9–12ft) in length and are usually used with slightly heavier lines than those used with match or float rods. This is because they are used to cast weights ranging from 14–113g (½–4oz). A tip section, known as a quiver-tip is built into some rods. It has a very small diameter that flexes easily thereby registering when a fish has bitten. The quiver-tip's test curve is likely to be around 57–113g (2–4oz), while the main rod will have a test curve of between 453 and 680g (1lb and 1lb 8oz). Such rods are designed for use on quite fast-flowing rivers, while a quiver-tip of 14–28g (½–1oz) is more suited to still-water fishing. Leger or quiver-tip rods are used for catching a wide range of medium-weight coarse fish such as bream, tench, small carp and roach from still water, while in rivers barbel, chub and bream are the likely targets.

carp or pike rods

An ideal rod for fishing is the 907g (2lb) test curve carp or pike rod. Such a rod can be pushed into service for a vast range of species throughout the world and can be used for many differing purposes: landing bass, salmon, flounder, grey mullet, pollock and many other species of fish besides carp and pike.

Carp or pike rods are designed to cast weights from 14–113g (½–4oz) over medium to long distances. They have a test curve of between 680g and 1.8kg (1lb 8oz and 4lb) and a length that ranges between 3–4m (10–13ft). They vary in action, from tip action with a powerful mid section designed for distance casting, to soft, all-through action to tire fish out at close ranges as the rod absorbs their powerful lunges.

RIGHT THIS NEAR-TWENTY-POUND PIKE WAS CAUGHT USING A SHORT, SINGLE-HANDED BAIT-CASTING ROD.

ABOVE A SPINNING ROD LAUNCHES A LURE INTO A LAKE.

spinning or lure rods

Artificial lures are used mainly to catch predatory fish and spinning or lure rods are the tools for casting these lures. These rods range from 1.5–3.4m (5–11ft) in length and tend to have a fairly stiff action, because they need to transmit movement to the lure rather like a puppeteer transmits movement to a puppet. When a fish grabs the lure, the hook must take hold immediately because a fish does not hang on to a lure as it does with a natural bait.

There tends to be a big difference between lure rods designed for the American market and the European market (although these differences are starting to diminish as anglers explore each other's techniques). In the United States, anglers generally prefer short rods (called 'bait-casting' rods) which are used single-handed to cast lures for freshwater bass, northern pike and muskellunge. These rods and casting methods are now becoming widely used throughout Europe and the United Kingdom. English anglers have, however, traditionally preferred to use longer rods with which to cast their lures to salmon, pike and bass. Different lures work better with some rods than with others, which is why it is useful to own a range of spinning or lure rods. In lure fishing the rod is held throughout, from casting out to retrieving, and one can become very fond of a particular rod.

REELS

The reel's function is to store the line, to release the line on the cast and to retrieve the line when required. Reels intended for coarse fishing can be divided into four main categories: fixed-spool reels; closed-face reels; centrepin reels; and multiplier reels. In general, they all incorporate a braking system, generally referred to as 'a drag'. The drag setting is paramount when big fish are the target, as this uses friction to control the release of the line if a powerful fish is pulling hard enough to break it or pull the hook free. Additional braking can be applied using your thumb or a finger against the spool.

fixed-spool reels

As the name suggests a fixed-spool reel comprises a fixed spool with the line put onto this by a bale arm, which is driven by a series of gears operated by a reel handle. The spool is moved like a bobbin to ensure smooth lay of the line. When a cast is made, the bale arm is disengaged and the line is pulled from the spool's lip by the momentum of the weight being cast. Most good fixed-spool reels include an adjustable drag system: sometimes this is positioned in front of the reel but more often it takes the form of a knob behind the reel. The knob allows the 'slipping clutch' to be adjusted to a position so the reel 'gives' line when the bale arm is closed – this safety device helps to stop a hooked fish from snapping the line.

Most fixed-spool reels have what is called a 'line clip' on the side of the spool. This is used when you need to cast very accurately – but only when you are not expecting to catch fish that are big enough to break the line. You cast to your selected mark and wrap the line around the clip. The

ABOVE AND LEFT FIXED
SPOOL REELS.

next time you cast, try using a little more force and you'll find your cast has been stopped by the line clip and will be positioned at exactly the same distance out from the bank as your earlier cast.

Because they are relatively easy to use and are not prone to tangling, fixed-spool reels are ideal for novice anglers. The secret of trouble-free casting is to load the spool to its optimum level, generally around a 65mm (¼in) from the lip of the spool. The less line there is on the spool, the greater the resistance; and the further the weight flies, the greater the resistance, which can result in shortened distances.

This reel type is the number one choice for 90 per cent of all bait fishers for coarse fish species although fixed-spool reels are also used by a large number of sea anglers because they can cast bait a long way.

Tip
When you load a fixed-spool or closed-face reel, make sure that the line comes right to the edge of the spool: this reduces friction against the edge of the spool and makes for smoother and more accurate casting.

closed-face reels

With this type of reel, the spool is completely enclosed in a casing with only a small central hole through which the line emerges. Instead of a bale arm, closed-face reels are equipped with

BELOW THE BALE ARM LAYS LINE UPON THE SPOOL, WHICH MOVES BOBBIN-STYLE.

LEFT A CLASSIC CENTRE-PIN REEL.

a small pin around which the line is gathered inside the housing. Pressing gently on the front of the reel releases the spring-loaded pin and by trapping the line with a finger, you can cast in the same way as for a fixed-spool reel. A single turn of the handle re-engages the pin and you can then retrieve the line. Closed-face reels are not suited to catching big fish as the spool itself is usually quite narrow and shallow and best suited to light lines of no more than 1.1kg (2½lb) breaking strain. And while closed-face reels don't make long, accurate casts, they are nevertheless reliable and easy to use, and ideally suited to stick float fishing in windy weather. They are also good in environments where there is dense vegetation because grass and other debris don't get trapped in the spool.

centre-pin reels

This type of reel is the oldest design and has been used for thousands of years. Modern versions are made from machined aluminium, plastic or carbon fibre. Some centre-pin reels have solid-face drums, while others have a series of holes drilled into the face to reduce the weight of the reel. The centre-pin reel has a spool that revolves – as the name suggests – on a central pin. The line leaves the spool with a freedom that is unmatched by other forms of reel: a gentle tap on the drum of the reel will send it spinning for over a minute, but mastering control takes a lot more time, so they are not the best choice for a novice.

ABOVE THIS MULTIPLIER HAS
A LEVEL WIND TO ENSURE
GOOD LINE LAY.

Centre-pin reels are a delight to use when trotting rivers for roach, dace and grayling at close range. Combined with a long float rod (see page 28), a good-quality well-engineered centre-pin reel enables anglers to control their tackle with ease. Centre-pin reels are also used for close-range fishing for barbel and carp, when they provide direct contact with the fish. In addition, they allow anglers to prevent fish from reaching the sanctuary of 'snags' (trees or branches embedded in riverbeds) making them ideal for fishing in snaggy conditions.

multiplier reels

Kentucky watchmaker and silversmith, George Snyder, built the predecessor of the modern multiplier reel at the beginning of the 19th century (the first casting reels were often called Kentucky reels). Snyder designed and made a reel where the spool rotated around its axis several times for every turn of the handle. Modern multiplier reels work on the same principle: the spool turns around the central pin, but unlike a centre-pin reel, a multiplier reel has a gear system that allows for the speedy recovery of the line. To ensure smooth operation, and to give the potential to make long casts, the spool is mounted on ball bearings. The major difference between the multiplier and other types of reel is that it is attached to the top of the rod and so certain rods are designed slightly differently to accommodate multiplier reels: the rod rings are generally smaller and the reel seat is designed to give the most comfortable grip possible.

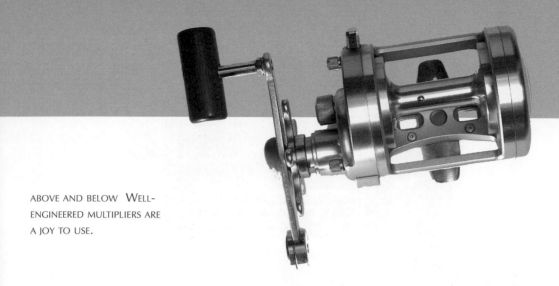

ABOVE AND BELOW WELL-ENGINEERED MULTIPLIERS ARE A JOY TO USE.

OPPOSITE TOP RIGHT THE THUMB CONTROLS THE REVOLVING SPOOL AS THE BAIT IS LOWERED TO THE SEABED.

OPPOSITE BOTTOM RIGHT A MULTIPLIER USED FOR DISTANCE BEACHCASTING: THE ANGLER USES A RUBBER STRIP TO IMPROVE GRIP DURING POWERFUL CASTS.

The multiplier is the reel of choice for most boat fishers out at sea and it is particularly suited to fishing for large species of fish such as shark, skate and marlin. Smaller multipliers are also widely used for bait-casting and bait-spinning: while there is no great difference in the distance that can be achieved compared to a fixed-spool reel, multiplier reels are great fun to use. The main drawback with multiplier reels – especially for beginners – is that they are prone to what are called 'bird's nests', in other words, the most dreadful tangles. Bird's nests occur when the weight that has been cast slows down

after its initial launch, but the spool is still spinning extremely fast following the initial acceleration powered by the cast. If the spool is not slowed down, it will continue to feed out line that is not needed and the result can be a nasty tangle of line. Many modern multipliers do now have sophisticated braking systems – either centrifugal or magnetic – that help to control the rotating spool during the cast, but they do tend to reduce casting distance.

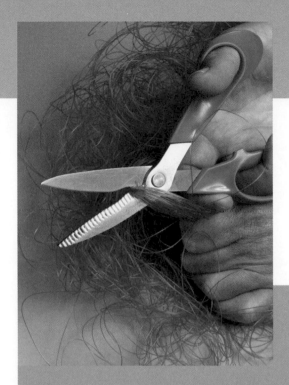

LEFT LINE SHOULD BE CUT INTO SHORT
LENGTHS BEFORE DISPOSAL AS IT CAN HARM
WILDLIFE.

LINES

The line is the vital connection between the angler's world and the mysterious world of the fish. Until the 1950s, fishing line was made from natural materials such as silk, cotton and horsehair. As natural fibres, these were prone to rotting and need careful drying after use while hook lengths had to be soaked prior to use to make them supple enough to be attached to the hook. In contrast, modern lines, as long as they are stored out of direct sunlight, will keep their strength for a long time. 'Fishing line' is something of a misnomer because there are many different types of line:

there are main lines and hook lengths; floating lines and sinking lines; braided and pre-stretched lines. Each type of line has a specific use so it is important to have a basic understanding of them.

Lines are rated in terms of breaking strain (bs) and diameter; some lines are stretchy others have little stretch. Some are soft, others less so with greater memory – in other words they retain twists from being stored on the reel.

The line you choose must be:
• Strong enough to land the type of fish that is likely to be hooked.
• Suitable for casting the required distance.
• Unlikely to scare the fish away from the bait.

ABOVE MONOFILAMENT LINE REVOLUTIONISED
THE ANGLING WORLD.

Tip
Once a knot has been put into a line – such as when tying on a hook link or a hook – the breaking strain (bs) of the line is greatly reduced. Many line manufacturers now indicate this on the spool as the 'knot strength'.

monofilament lines

The most commonly used line for coarse anglers is monofilament line made of nylon. A synthetic fibre, nylon was discovered by DuPont in 1937 and at first was received with great scepticism by anglers who were used to natural fibre lines. The nylon fibre is made by extruding it through holes of different diameters after which the threads are cooled and then drawn across heated and rotating wheels to stretch and align the molecules so they become stiffer, stronger and less elastic.

Today 'mono', as anglers call it, comes in many variations and different qualities: some 'mono' lines float – ideal for float fishing – while others are designed to sink, making it ideal for legering. As well

as being available in a range of colours, mono is quite strong, can stretch and is generally the right choice for the main line to put on the reel.

The big disadvantage of this line is its potential to inflict harm on wildlife if it is left carelessly on a bank or shoreline: even disposed of in a waste bin, it may end up in a landfill site where birds may become entangled in it. This is why it's best to burn the line or cut it up into short lengths before disposing of it.

Tip
For float fishing, a 0.9–1.36kg (2–3lb) breaking strain would be a good choice, while for legering, 1.36–1.8kg (3–4lb) breaking strain mono is recommended. Big carp and pike anglers need a more substantial main line of no less than 4.54kg (10lb).

pre-stretched lines

Some lines are pre-stretched in order to reduce their diameter: the thinner the line, the less obvious it is to the fish. These have a high breaking strain for their diameter compared with mono main lines, but because much of their 'stretch' has already been removed, they can be quite brittle and aren't suitable, therefore, for use as main lines. Instead they are better used for hook links or as main lines on pole rigs, where the pole's elastic – a short length of elastic line – provides a 'shock absorber'.

Many articles on angling now refer to the diameter of a line in millimetres (e.g. 0.12mm) rather than its strength: these are invariably referring to pre-stretched lines and, while different makes have different breaking strains (bs), the following table gives a general idea of these:

Diameter of Line	Breaking Strain (bs)
0.07mm	453g (1lb)
0.08mm	680g (1lb 8oz)
0.09mm	907g (2lb)
0.10mm	1.13kg (2lb 8oz)
0.12mm	1.36kg (3lb)
0.14mm	1.81kg (4lb)
0.16mm	2.26kg (5lb)

braided main line

Braided lines are a weave of materials – a bit like extremely thin rope – and can be used for main lines and hook links: main line braids are generally supplied in spools of at least 100m (300ft), while hook link braids usually come on spools of 10–20m (33–66ft).

Manufactured from materials such as Kevlar – the fibre that is used to make bulletproof vests – braided line has had a great impact on angling. Such lines have even thinner diameters than nylon monofilament and have very little stretch. This lack of stretch provides a far superior bite indication and can lead to longer casts. In lure fishing it also gives the angler an excellent feeling of how the lure is working and enables hooks to be driven home into fishes' mouths with minimum effort.

When using braided lines, it's important to increase the breaking strain (bs) used, firstly to allow for the lack of stretch (which can result in its sudden failure) and secondly, to minimise the potential loss of expensive terminal tackle and lures. Care must also be exercised when the end tackle becomes entangled (snagged) in some unseen rock or debris: you'll need to pull the line until the lure breaks. Doing this with bare hands can result in nasty cuts, so wear gloves or wrap the lure around a suitable piece of smooth wood. Remember, too, that braided lines present the same environmental hazards as nylon monofilament (but braided lines do last longer – sometimes for more than one season).

hook links, lengths or traces

In addition to the main line, you need to use a hook link – sometimes known as a hook length or a trace. These may sometimes be part of the main line, but it is more often a separate section of line that attaches the hook to the main line. Hook links must be less than the strength of the main line: as a general rule, the hook link's breaking strain should be 10–20 per cent less than that of your main line so, if you snag up, or the fish breaks free, you only lose the hook link and not metres of line trailing behind.

The optimum length of the hook link is determined by several factors including the water conditions, the species of fish anticipated, the terrain and the angling pressure. In clear water conditions, the fish are likely to be aware of a visible line: here it might be advisable to use a hook link with as light a breaking strain as possible. In freshwater bait-fishing, a hook link of clear mono line is a good choice although fluorocarbon line is also valuable, because its light-reflective properties greatly reduce its visibility under water.

If the targeted species of fish has sharp teeth or an abrasive mouth (like a large proportion of predatory fish), you will need a wire trace. Remember that it is the angler's responsibility always to choose tackle that is strong enough to land any fish likely to bite. In waters that contain several different predatory species it may be necessary to use a wire in case you hook a species not directly targeted.

If fishing for perch using small live bait or spinners in a water containing pike, for example, a wire trace is essential, even if it reduces the chances of catching perch. The wire trace that you choose depends on the species and size of fish targeted. Care must be taken with wire, which weakens if it becomes kinked or corroded.

Terrain also determines the strength and characteristics of the hook link. Rocks or gravel

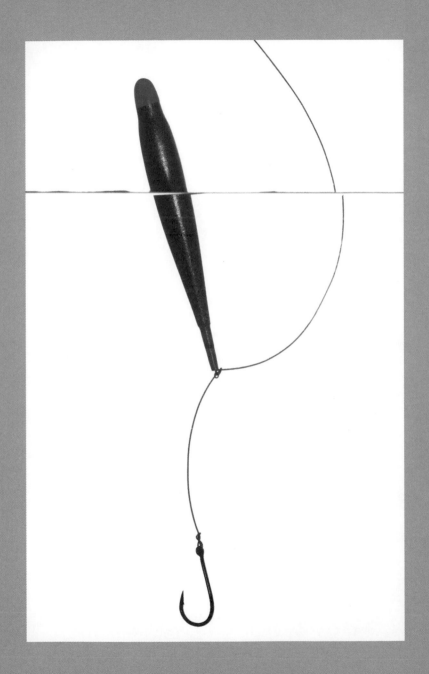

are likely to fray the line, so a heavier and thicker line is required. If there are fallen trees or other such fish havens present, a strong line is needed to prevent the fish from reaching them.

Angling pressure – where fish are targeted by a large number of anglers – also influences the choice of hook link. In many coarse fishing venues, the fish are caught and returned to the water many times and fish such as carp and barbel are capable of developing a cunning that enables them to detect lines and hook links. A wide range of special hook links has been developed to counteract this problem and enhance the presentation of the bait.

Braided hook links are softer and more flexible than the braids used for main lines and they have a very small diameter in relation to their strength (compared to mono). Although this makes braided hook links more expensive than mono versions, the combination of softness and thinness, as well as a high degree of abrasion resistance, appeals to anglers fishing for cautious fish in snaggy swims.

ABOVE CRAB FISHING LINES.

HOOKS

The hook is the final link in the chain between angler and fish, its purpose being to hold the bait and secure the fish. Early hooks were made of wood or bone. Some were gorge hooks that wedged into the fish's throat – unacceptable in today's conservation-minded world.

Most of today's hooks are made from tempered steel wire and have seven major features: the eye, shank, bend, gape, throat, barb and point. These features themselves can also vary in shape and description, bearing names such as 'hollow point', 'needle eye', kirbed shank' and 'reversed point'. In general, the names are useful descriptions: a 'round eye' is exactly that, while a 'tapered eye' hook has tapered wire for its eye. Hooks with curved points are usually used with natural bait, while hooks with straight points are used for spinning with artificial lures.

BELOW A TYPICAL HOOK.

shank

eye

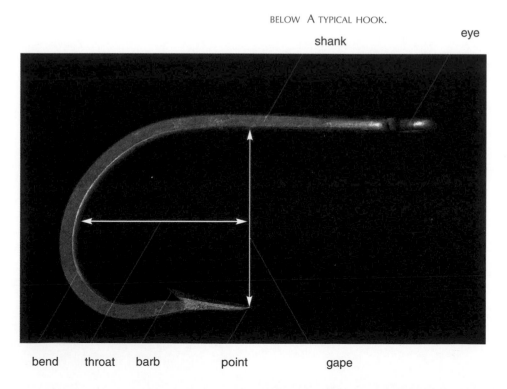

bend   throat   barb   point   gape

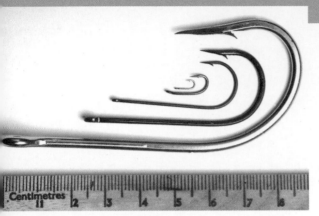

LEFT HOOK SIZES 22 UP TO 12/0.

There are hundreds of different hook 'patterns' on the market, with varying shanks lengths and curves, and manufacturers have begun to identify on the packet the type of angling to which the hook is best suited – a bonus for beginners.

hook size

Generally recognised hook sizes are based on the Redditch scale, where the size of hooks are denoted by a number: although sizes may vary between manufacturers, in general, the smallest coarse fishing hooks start at no.30 and increase in size to no.1. In simple terms, you should be fishing small, fine, wire hooks – around sizes 18–22 with small baits (such as pinkies or maggots) for small fish (such as roach and dace).

The bigger the fish you are after, the bigger the hook you'll need as fine wire hooks are easily bent or snapped by larger, hard-fighting fish. You might then choose a size 10–12 for a chub and a size 4–8 for a carp. There are also double and treble hooks: these are effectively a combination of two or three hooks to create greater hooking power. Treble hooks are widely used on lures to achieve a more effective hook-up ratio (doubles are used for the same reason in some flies) and to present fish bait to pike and other predatory species of fish.

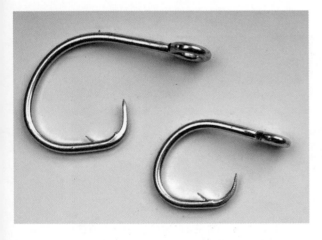

ABOVE CIRCLE HOOKS CATCH FISH IN THE SIDE OF THE MOUTH SO THEY CAN BE RETURNED UNHARMED.

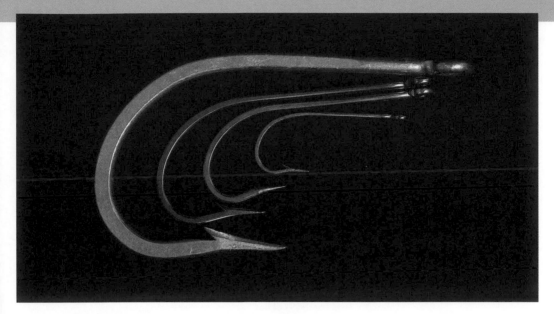

ABOVE HOOKS VARY GREATLY IN DESIGN.

hook strength

The strength of a hook is derived in the main from the gauge of the wire used: the thicker the gauge, the stronger the hook. Increasingly, however, manufacturers are marking the packaging with useful indicators such as 'forged', 'x-strong' and 'carp' to help in their identification.

The temper of wire determines the use a hook may be put to. While fine wire hooks penetrate more easily, they are also more prone to straightening during a battle with a large specimen. On the other hand, a fine wire hook will also be lighter and present bait more naturally: fish are not stupid and even small fish can be very wary of a thick piece of wire protruding from a tasty bait. Fish that have been caught and returned to the water several times begin to associate the shape of the hook with danger. The smaller and finer the hook, the less likely the fish are to see or feel it. The ideal hook is light, strong and able to maintain a secure hold within the mouth of the fish. Careful heating of the carbon steel used to make the hook determines the brittleness: a hook that breaks suddenly is a waste of time while a certain amount of flexibility has to be incorporated into the hook's shank and bend.

Hooks should always be carefully inspected before use for any sign of weakness or corrosion as well as to ensure that their points are

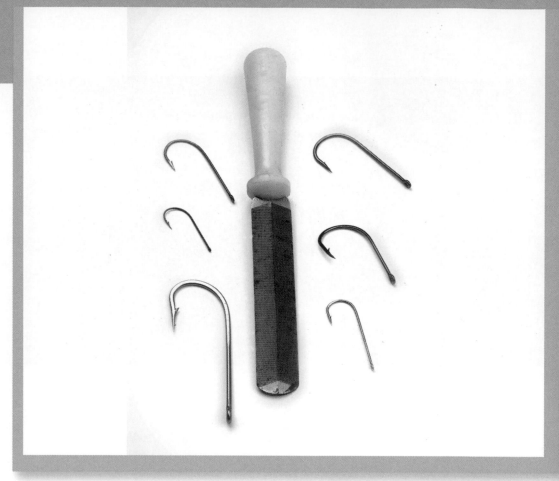

ABOVE A HOOK FILE IS ESSENTIAL FOR KEEPING
NON-CHEMICALLY SHARPENED HOOKS SHARP.

extremely sharp. Once the point has become dulled or blunted – by rubbing against stones, for example – a sharpening stone is needed to restore the point. Many modern hooks are now chemically sharpened (this is indicated on the label), a process that produces an exceptionally sharp point, but once these have become dull or blunt, it's impossible to restore the point.

eyed and spade end hooks

Hooks can also be either 'eyed' – attached to the line with a knot through the eye – or 'spade end', which have to be attached with a whipping knot on the hook's shank. The standard knot used for attaching an eyed hook is a tucked half-blood knot that is quite easy to tie. Tying spade end knots is a bit trickier, but fortunately it is now possible to buy packets of pre-tied spade end hooks called

RIGHT TREBLE HOOKS, WIDELY USED ON LURES.

'hooks to nylon', which can be attached to the main line using a four-turn water knot, another easy knot to tie.

barbed, barbless and microbarb hooks

Hooks can be barbed, barbless or have a microbarb. The purpose of the barb is to hold a live bait, such as a maggot or worm, on the hook and to prevent the fish shaking itself free. This will only work if the hook has penetrated beyond the barb – which is why a big barb is not desirable. The barb of a hook is often a bone of contention amongst anglers and many freshwater anglers use barbless hooks to reduce damage to fish that are to be returned (indeed this is mandatory on many waters). By keeping a tight line between the rod and the fish when playing it, barbless hooks are just as suitable as barbed hooks. Microbarb hooks, as the name suggests, have a tiny barb just below the point and are generally used for pole fishing.

WEIGHTS

Once the line has been cast, the weight carries the bait and the hook to their destination and then keeps the bait there. The weight can also be used to assist in the hooking of a fish by creating an anchor point that pulls the hook into place within the fish's jaws. Additionally, the weight is used in float fishing to 'cock the float' (so that only a little piece of the tip is visible above the water) and sink the bait to the desired level.

Until recently, most weights were made of lead on account of its heaviness but environmental concerns have forced manufacturers to offer weights at smaller sizes in alternative materials, so now most weights under 28g (1oz) and are lead free. Each weight is designed for a specific purpose so the choice of weight is determined by the particular situation facing the angler. In many instances, the location of the fish determines the weight needed (and consequently the rod with which to cast it). Many of the weights available are designed for carp fishing with some designed primarily for

achieving distance while others are designed to cling to the riverbed in running water or a steep-sided lake.

split shot and olivettes

The smallest weights used by anglers are called split shots and are used when float fishing for smaller species, for giving weight to bait when free lining, or using a light leger. Split shot range in size from the tiny dust shot (about the size of a pinhead) to swan shot, which is about the size of a pea. The sizes are indicated from largest to smallest: SSG, SG, AAA, AA, BB, 1, 4, 6, 8, 9, 10, 11, 12, 13 and 14. The larger sizes are placed around the base of a float to make up about four-fifths of the total weight required, with smaller shots – such as size 8s – strung out below. In pole fishing, most of the weight is concentrated in a bulk about two-thirds of the way down the line with a couple of tiny shots strung out below.

Instead of using shots for the bulk, you can buy olivettes: these are more streamlined in form

RIGHT SPLIT SHOT IS ATTACHED TO THE LINE BY PINCHING IT CAREFULLY IN PLACE.

TOP RIGHT A SELECTION OF WEIGHTS USED BY THE FRESHWATER ANGLER.

OPPOSITE SPLIT SHOT – SSG (LEFT) AND NUMBER 6 (RIGHT).

than shots and are measured in grams. For general legering, a small bomb-type weight is used, namely the Arlesey-type weight. The original was designed by the late Richard Walker for perch fishing on the Arlesey Lake in the 1950s, and this now forms the basis for most of the weights used for casting at any distance in both fresh and salt water.

Some weights have been designed to carry loose feed or groundbait to the area being that is being fished. Swimfeeders are weighted cylinders full of holes that are filled with bait or groundbait. There are two basic types of swimfeeder: open-end and block-end. Open-end feeders are plugged with groundbait that disperses in the water, while block-end feeders have sealed ends so that the loose feed, typically maggots, escapes through the holes. A third type of feeder called a method feeder is also widely used. This weight is designed to allow a paste-like groundbait to be moulded around it, producing a ball of bait that slowly dissolves to form an appetising mound beside the hook.

FLOATS

Floats generally serve two purposes: firstly, to indicate a bite and, secondly, to suspend the bait at the desired depth beneath the surface. The prevailing conditions, along with the type of bait and tackle being used, determines the size of the float.

There are floats designed for still water, windy weather, rivers, poles, pike fishing and so on and there are wagglers, stick floats, loafers, pencils, dibbers, balsas, toppers, Avons and sliders to choose from. If these aren't enough, there are floats with wire stems and cane bristles, cane stems and nylon bristles, carbon stems and cane bristles!

All are designed for specific situations and different types of fishing, but understanding a basic range of floats is the best starting point for the beginner.

stick floats

Stick floats are designed for use in running water and can be made of cane (for close-in work), lignum (for longer casting distances) or be wire stemmed, for use in turbulent water. These floats are attached to the line by soft, hollow rings of silicone in what is called a 'top and bottom' manner. Put simply, this means that the line from the rod is fastened to the top of the float but it allows the angler greater control of the behaviour of the float as it runs downstream so the float can be slowed down or even brought to a standstill against the water's flow. Doing this, the angler can 'tease' the bait and alter its presentation to the fish, tempting them to bite.

TOP RIGHT A THREE-WAY SWIVEL GIVES THREE POINTS OF ATTACHMENT.

BOTTOM RIGHT SWIVELS CONNECT LINES AND REDUCE TWIST.

wagglers

These floats are attached to the line through a ring at the bottom end (unlike the stick float attached at the top), and locked in position by a split shot at either end. Further bits of shot are then added until only about 1.25cm (½in) of the bright tip of the waggler is visible above the surface film of the water. Loaded wagglers are also available: these carry weight pre-loaded in the base of the float, so less shot is needed to cock them in the water. Wagglers are used on both still and flowing water with different types operating best in different depths but, as a basic rule, the further you need to cast and the deeper the water, the heavier the waggler you need.

pole and pike floats

There are numerous pole floats available on the market. The majority are attached to the line by two small, silicone bands on the body of the float with the line passing through an eye in the upper half. Some pole floats are called 'body up'. These are floats with a bulbous body close to the top of the stem and are designed for use in running water. If the float is 'body down' then it is designed for use in still water. Furthermore, wire- and carbon-stemmed pole floats are used for fishing on the bottom, while cane-stemmed pole floats are used for fishing 'on the drop' or in the upper 'layers' of water. Bigger than wagglers, pole or stick floats, pike floats are often hollow so the line can be threaded through: the float then slides up and down the line until it meets a small stopper knot set to match the depth of water. Pike floats are specially designed to be extra buoyant to allow a fish to be suspended underneath without sinking.

It is important that a float is weighted correctly: ideally only a small portion of the float should be visible above the water 'Cocking the float' so that just the very tip is visible ensures that the fish feels little resistance when taking the bait and, if a fish's suspicions are not aroused, the angler has more time to respond to its presence and set the hook.

SWIVELS

A swivel's primary function is to connect two sections of line. It also helps to reduce twisting of the line and therefore improves the presentation of the bait. In many instances the swivel also acts as a stop to prevent a weight or a float from sliding downwards and becoming entangled with the bait. (The only branch of fishing in which the use of swivels is uncommon is fly-fishing). Swivels are rated in size much in the way that hooks are and it is important to select a swivel that is much stronger than the line being used. There are also terminal tackle set-ups available that incorporate three-way swivels that give three points of attachment: to the main line, to the hook and to the weight.

ABOVE HOMEMADE DROP-OFF INDICATORS SUITABLE FOR PIKE FISHING.

It's worth spending a bit more money on a good-quality swivel: a failure in a poor-quality swivels can lead to the loss of a big fish or people in the vicinity being injured during a powerful cast.

BITE INDICATORS

In pole fishing, quiver-tip rods and floats are the primary bite indicators, but there are also 'glow in the dark' floats designed for night fishing. When legering, there are various forms of bite indicators to choose from. Once again, selection depends on the fish you are targeting.

butt-style indicators

Butt-style indicators are the most commonly used indicator for specimen angling. Traditionally, silver paper (usually milk bottle tops), a cork or a piece of bread dough was moulded around the main line and allowed to hang below the rod, but today there are state-of-the-art indicators with easy-release line clip, luminous inserts and adjustable weightings or sensitivity. These indicators are normally in the form of a bobbin of some type and are fitted between the reel and rings near the butt of the rod. When a fish takes the bait and pulls on the line, the indicator will either rise or fall,

depending on the direction in which the fish moves away or on the set-up of the terminal tackle being used. In many instances, butt indicators are used with audible alarms that emit a 'beep' when the fish picks up the bait and takes the line, while for night fishing, there are LED light alarms so the angler can see which rod has a 'run'.

swing tips

Swing tips are attached to rods in a similar manner to quiver tips, but instead of following the 'line' of the rod, a flexible insert of silicone close to the attachment causes the swing tip to 'hang down'. The angler casts in and sets the tip so it hangs downwards at 90 degrees from the end of the rod. A bite is indicated when the tip moves towards the rig or drops back. In still waters swing tips are ideal and are often used for fishing bream and roach, because they offer very little tension detectable to the fish. Swing tips are not suited to running water though: the flow straightens out the tip and consequently makes bite detection impossible.

swingers and springers

These are more advanced bite indicators used for carp fishing. Swingers attach to the front bank stick, just underneath the bite alarm. An

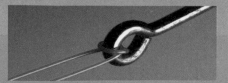

1. Thread the line through the hook eye twice.

2. Form a large loop through which to pass the end of the line.

3. Pass the end of the line through the loop five times.

4. Begin to pull the knot tight carefully.

5. Wet the line with saliva and continue to tighten the knot.

6. Trim off the tag end. (A tag end can be left to help hold bait in position.)

7. The completed knot.

arm hangs down – an isotope, starlight or other luminous indicator can be attached here to a clip fitted at the end and into which the main line also clips. The weight on the swinging arm can be adjusted to suit wind speeds and the line is released from the clip when the angler strikes. Springers hold the line under tension and 'spring off' the line when the fish takes the bait.

KNOTS

There is no use buying the best tackle money can buy if you have not learned the basic skill of tying knots. Knots are required to connect the line to the terminal tackles, such as hooks and swivels, as well as to the reel spool, and to join two lines together. It's vital that knots are tied correctly, as badly or incorrectly tied knots can slip and untie. Nothing is more frustrating to an angler after putting great effort into hooking a fish than to lose it because of an inadequate knot.

Although there are a vast number of knots used in angling, to start off with you only need to become familiar with a few of the most useful. These are the grinner (shown above); the tucked

ABOVE A ROD POD SUPPORTS A PAIR OF RODS.

half blood knot; the loop; the water knot; the blood knot (for joining together lines of equal diameter); the leader knot; the knotless hook attachment; and the stop knot. You can practise tying them in 'small stuff' (string or thin rope) first to become familiar with technique and pattern before tying them in mono or braid.

ACCESSORIES

Some accessories are needed for certain types of fishing, but there are also accessories designed to make angling more comfortable. Not all are necessary to start with and you can build up your 'tackle collection' over time, customising it to suit your preferred type of fishing.

rod rests

A rod rest is an essential item for all types of angling but the type of rest depends upon the required position of the rod and the type of method being used. For simple float fishing for example, the rod is placed upon a rest and positioned close at hand so that the angler can strike instantly on receiving an indication of a bite. Anglers using quiver-tip rods need to position the rod at an angle to the water, supported by a front and rear rest, again in a position that allows the angler to react immediately.

If the angler is legering using a butt indicator, the rod should be pointed in the direction of the main line as it enters the water. Front and rear rests are essential and the front rest (which may incorporate an audible alarm) must allow enough space for the main line to pass through unimpeded.

The front and rear rests need to be strong enough to support the rod in strong winds and to stop the rod from being pulled into the water when a big fish takes the bait. If a bank consists of stone or concrete and the bank stick on the rod rest cannot be driven into the ground, a rod pod is required.

ABOVE A PAIR OF PLIERS IS USEFUL FOR REMOVING HOOKS FROM LARGE FISH.

ABOVE THIS HOOK IS EASY TO REMOVE WITH A SIMPLE DISGORGER.

ABOVE THIS LARGE PERCH HAS BEEN PHOTOGRAPHED ON AN UNHOOKING MAT.

RIGHT LOADED UP WITH TACKLE.

This is a platform that allows the rod (or rods) to be rested in the correct position. Rod pods, which are widely used by carp anglers, have the advantage that they can be carried easily from swim to swim (the pools in rivers that provide good fishing).

disgorgers

When you have landed a fish, you then need to extract the hook. You can do this quickly and safely with the help of a disgorger. The type of disgorger you need depends on the type of fish, its dentition and where it has been hooked. A micro-disgorger is needed for hooks of size 22 or smaller, and a 'normal' sized one for hooks between sizes 14 and 20, but you can get disgorgers with a micro and a normal size at either end. The best ones are made of plastic – they float!

landing nets and keepnets

Once you've got the fish to the side of the water, you will only be able to lift it directly if it is a small specimen: lifting larger fish puts pressure on the hook and could break the line. Landing nets are available in a wide range: for river fishing, choose a landing net with a wide mesh so that the water passes through it easily and won't drag the net out of your hands when you try to land the fish. Fine-meshed landing nets are designed for still waters, but you need to select the right shaped net for the type of fish you are planning to catch: shallow 'pan' nets are best suited to canal fishing, or a deeper version for bigger species like tench and carp. The actual shape of the net – round, triangular or oval – is simply a matter of preference. Large specimen landing nets are also available: these can be really enormous and are for the very big

catfish, carp and pike angler. As with landing nets, there is a wide variety of keepnets available: one around 3m (10ft) long with a fine mesh and a locking device that works at different angles is a good choice to begin with. (Note that, in the UK, it is illegal to use knotted nets: all nets used in freshwater fishing must be constructed without knots to avoid damaging a fish's scales.)

unhooking mats

Gravel and hard banks can severely damage a fish that is flapping around on the ground: the essential slime that covers the fish, and its scales, can be damaged and an unhooking mat will protect it while you remove the hook. You can buy unhooking mats, but equally serviceable is a large piece of bubble wrap plastic or a sheet of plastic-covered padded foam. Using an unhooking mat is mandatory in many fisheries.

tackle carriers and seat boxes

Once you've acquired all the tackle you need, you'll now have to carry it all to the water's edge. You need something large enough to carry everything you need, that is easy to transport, and able to protect the contents from damage. While a rucksack or backpack can suffice, a better choice might be a plastic seat box: they are comfortable to carry (and many have wheels that make trundling along roads and banksides even less of an effort); they have plenty of room inside for tackle and if you have levelling legs added, you get the bonus of a tackle carrier that doubles as a comfortable seat.

shelters

The most common form of shelter is the angler's umbrella. This can be securely anchored to the banks with guy ropes so it doesn't blow away. Long-stay anglers might prefer a tent or 'bivvy' (bivouac) to house them and their gear: these range from the basic tent to those equipped with lights, televisions and even angler's showers.

ABOVE SUCCESS, THE FISH IS SAFELY IN THE NET.

BELOW THE BIVVY — ESSENTIAL FOR LONG-STAY ANGLERS.

food

Being out and about in the open air and angling for a couple hours works up an appetite: for short sessions an insulated flask with a hot drink or soup and box of doorstep sandwiches is essential. On longer sessions you might want a more civilised (or more substantial!) approach to dining al fresco: portable gas camp stoves, a kettle, cutlery – the choice is yours, but remember you have to carry it! And take a box of matches too: the electronic 'spark' lighting mechanisms on many modern camping stoves can be very temperamental. Whatever your style, make sure you pack it all up at the end of your fishing – along with any litter – and take it home.

Bait can be divided into three main categories: natural, manufactured and artificial. Each species of fish responds better to a particular bait, and the way it is presented. Fishing in heavily coloured water might need a big, smelly bait to attract fish, while, in clear water, a small, visible bait may be more productive. The best advice is to keep on experimenting with different baits: like us, fish feed differently from one day to another, so a fish that bites on something one day may not do so the next!

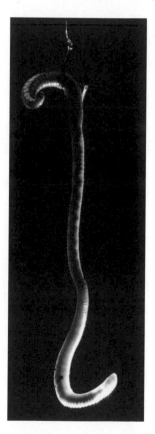

ABOVE WHAT FISH COULD RESIST THIS TASTY OFFERING?

ABOVE Maggots.

ABOVE It is important to ensure that the hook point is not masked by the bait.

NATURAL BAIT

worms

There are several varieties of worm for the angler to choose from: but the lobworm, or night crawler, is the most commonly used for large fish and can be dug up from the garden (or bought from tackle shops). Hook them through the head using size 8–12 hooks and store them carefully in a bait box of damp moss, newspaper, grass clippings or even the soil in which they were dug up. Dendrobaenas –

middle-sized worms – are good feeder bait when chopped and added to the water or when added to ground bait. On hooks – use size 10–16 – use them hooked at the cut end. Red worms can be found in compost heaps: bream love them, especially if tipped with a tasty maggot!

maggots

Maggots – the larvae of bluebottle flies – are probably the most widely used bait in coarse fishing. Most tackle shops sell them and they can

be bought in a variety of colours including white, red and bronze (a colour that is popular among many river anglers). Maggots are sold in measures of pints and half-pints and, when fresh, they have a large black spot near their 'pointed' end. They should be hooked through the 'blunt' end using a hook sized between 16 and 20. You can also buy spray-on flavours ranging from sweet to savoury to make them more tasty. To stop maggots from turning into casters (chrysalises) you need to keep them cool, ideally in a fridge. This might not go down well with other members of your family so invest in a dedicated bait fridge! Casters do have a

value as long as their shells remain pink: they readily sink in water (they float when they turn brown) and are used to attract fish –especially roach – in the swim. Thread the caster around the hook's bend (size 16–18) so the whole hook is buried inside the caster's shell.

pinkies

These are the larvae of greenbottle flies and are about half the size of a maggot. As their name suggests, they are pink in colour, but they too can be bought in different colours including

'flouro pink'. Pinkies are a good alternative to maggots when targeting small or shy biting fish and are hooked the same way as for maggots but onto size 18–22 hooks. Pinkies sink more slowly in water than maggots so aren't really useful for loose feeding in deep water.

squats

Smaller than pinkies, squats are the larvae of houseflies and are usually sold in damp, red sand. They are used for very small fish in canals (on hook sizes 20–26) and for packing into ground bait for 'balling in' or for fishing through an open-ended ground bait swimfeeder.

Tip
Maggots and pinkies escape when wet: if it starts to rain, make sure the lid on their container is tightly sealed.

bread

Bread is cheap but effective bait that can be presented in a variety of ways – as flake, crust and paste. Flake is just a piece of fresh bread whose centre is squeezed onto a hook – the size of hook will depend on the size of the flake. For small species like roach, a thumbnail-sized flake on a size 10 hook works well; for bigger fish, like carp, a flake the size of a walnut on a size 4 hook is needed. You can also use a bread punch. Available in sets with different sized heads, these allow you to punch neatly formed pellets from fresh, white bread: using a size 14–22 hook, push the point down through the slot at the side of the punch and turn the hook to secure the pellet.

Roughly torn pieces of fresh white bread are good for carp fishing in warm weather on still, dark summer nights. A few pieces scattered onto the surface of the water – crust floats nicely – will bring carp to feed. Keeping yourself well concealed, offer a crust on a size 6–4 hook into the margins of the water, and the bait should be taken. Smaller fish, such as chub and rudd, also take floating crusts: use size 10 or 12 hooks with a thumbnail-sized crust bait.

Paste is an excellent bait for chub, carp, tench and barbel, and is made from a white loaf – about four or five days old and with the crusts removed. The bread is soaked in water until nice and soggy and the water squeezed out to leave a doughy mass. You can add all manner of flavours (and colours) to this – try cheese or soft fruit – by kneading it into the bread. If you don't want to make your own paste, you can buy ready prepared varieties (you just add water). Whichever you choose, the paste should be firm enough to stay on the hook during casting, but soft enough to come off the hook as you strike at the bite. If your paste is too soft, you can always firm it up by mixing in some dry flour.

Hook it on so that the paste covers the whole of the hook bend and shank, leaving the tip visible: hooks from size 6–14 are ideal for bread paste.

Tips

Breadcrumbs are often used as the bulk ingredient for groundbait. They form a cloud in the water that stimulates the fish without over-feeding them.

Stale bread can be soaked, placed into a bucket and mashed, either by hand or with a potato masher. The mashed bread can then be thrown into the swim by hand or in a cage feeder.

Fresh bread can be made into perfect ground bait by placing in a food processor and

liquidising it into tiny particles. These particles can then be squeezed into balls and either thrown into the swim, or squeezed around a method-style feeder prior to casting.

BELOW BOILIES ARE THE MOST WIDELY USED MODERN CARP BAIT.

groundbait

In its simplest form, groundbait is dried and crushed bread (anglers call it crumb), which is used to attract fish into the swim and keep them in a tight area on the bottom – or very close to the bottom. The crumb is mixed with water – the drier the mix, the faster it will break up on contact with the water – and moulded into small balls. These are either thrown by hand, shot with a catapult or placed in an open-ended feeder. You can add flavours in liquid or powder form: sweet flavours are best in summer, while spicy ones are preferred in winter. Or you can buy ready made 'secret recipe' mixes, some of which are designed (and labelled as such) to attract particular species or for using in different fishing venues: on fast-flowing rivers you need the ground bait to stay together so that it falls to the bottom, while on still water a lighter mix is needed that starts to break up as soon as it hits the water.

boilies

A boilie (see right) is a paste bait that has been immersed in boiling water. The ingredients can vary – bread, semolina or ground-up trout pellets are often used, bound together with egg, and coloured and flavoured before being moulded into balls of different sizes. Boiling them leaves a hard crust, which makes them resistant to small fish and allows them to stay in the swim for long periods before breaking down. You can buy base mixes from tackle

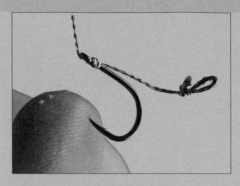

1. HOOK AND HAIR RIG LOOP.

2. INSERT BAITING NEEDLE INTO BAIT.

3. PUSH CAREFULLY THROUGH LEAVING POINT AND BARB SHOWING.

shops or ready-made versions that are sized in millimetres by their diameter.

4. ATTACH LOOP TO BARB AND PULL THROUGH BAIT.

5. THE BAITING NEEDLE IS REMOVED.

6. INSERT A BAIT STOP INTO LOOP.

7. PULL TIGHT AND TRIM OFF BAIT STOP.

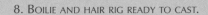

8. BOILIE AND HAIR RIG READY TO CAST.

ABOVE HEMP SEED IS A BRILLIANT ATTRACTOR.

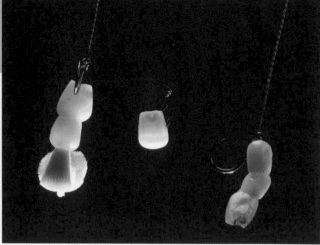

ABOVE SWEETCORN CAN BE PRESENTED ON A HOOK IN VARIOUS WAYS.

BELOW THE TOP ROW DISPLAYS SOFT PLASTIC LURES THAT WILL TEMPT A WIDE RANGE OF PREDATORY FISH, INCLUDING BASS AND PIKE; THOSE IN THE SECOND ROW ARE MORE SUITABLE FOR PERCH OR CHUB; THE BOTTOM TWO ROWS ARE RUBBER EELS SUITABLE FOR BASS, POLLOCK AND COD OVER REEFS OR WRECKS.

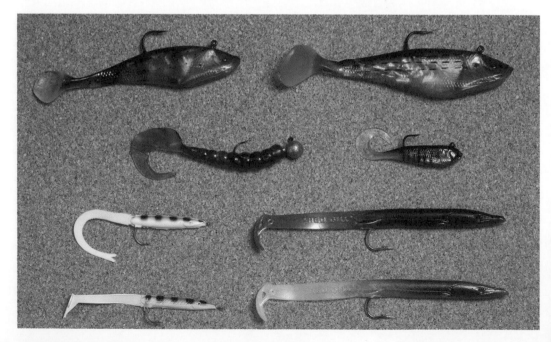

ABOVE SPINNER BAITS ARE A VARIATION ON THE TRADITIONAL SPINNER.

RIGHT A SMALL PIKE THAT ATTACKED A SPINNER BAIT.

In addition to the above baits, sweetcorn, cheese, processed meat and dog biscuits are all valuable baits. Sweetcorn can be used straight from the tin and is good bait for fishing for carp in summer: cover as much of the hook's shank as possible, leaving the point free. Use one piece of sweetcorn on a size 16 hook, two pieces on a size 12, and so on as the hook size increases. Soft cheese works well when mixed into pastes, while rubbery cheese stays well on the hook: cut the cheese into cubes and attach to hook sizes 6–12, with the hook pointing out. Some of the more smelly cheeses are ideal for attracting fish on rivers in flow conditions. Chub, barbel and carp seem to be attracted by processed meat (like luncheon meat) fished in cubes on hair rigs or directly on the hook, while other fish have a taste for cat food (especially the fish varieties!) and hotdog sausages. Dog biscuits float well and make good summer bait for carp and chub.

BELOW A SPINNER CONSISTS OF A BLADE THAT REVOLVES AROUND A CENTRAL SHAFT.

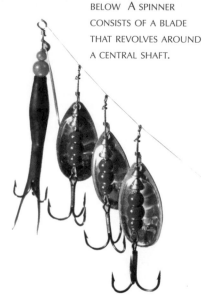

ABOVE MACKEREL IS A FINE BAIT FOR PIKE

ABOVE THIS BROWN TROUT ATTACKED THE LIVE BAIT THAT WAS INTENDED FOR PERCH.

RIGHT DEAD BAITS CAN BE INJECTED WITH FLAVOURS TO ENHANCE THEIR APPEAL.

While they can be flavoured and coloured they are difficult to attach to a hook: score a groove down one side of the biscuit and glue the back side of a size 10–12 hook to it with a 'super' bonding glue.

dead bait

Dead bait is exactly that: dead fish that are offered to predators like pike, perch and catfish. As these fish get older and bigger, they also get a little less nimble and less inclined to chase after live fish, preferring instead to scavenge for dead fish on the bottom. You can buy dead bait from tackle shops (where it can be bought in different colours) as well as in their 'natural' state at local fishmongers. Herring make effective pike bait (because they look most like roach, the predator's preferred meal) but mackerel and roach are also good. Sardines (not tinned ones, as they're too soft), sprats and peeled shrimps and prawns make tasty bait too.

Artificial lures are designed to imitate the fish that predatory species feed on. They need little preparation – you don't need to collect bait for example – so are ideal for anglers with limited time or for those 'spur of the moment' fishing trips. For most freshwater fishing you can choose from a variety of plugs and spinners: plugs 'wobble' through the water with an upright motion while spinners have a blade that rotates around an axis to create a spinning action.

The majority of plugs are made from a single piece of painted wood, coloured plastic or metal. There are three varieties: surface plugs (also known as poppers), floating divers and sinking divers. Most surface plugs don't, in fact, look like anything a predatory fish would naturally take, but the vibrations they transmit across the surface of the water triggers a response in the fish, which mistakes the plug for a small fish or even a frog swimming. Surface plugs are best used close to lily beds and reed lines in under 3m (10 ft) of clear water.

Floating divers (known as 'cranks' in the US) can be fished along the surface on a slow retrieve or made to dive under the surface by retrieving the line quickly (called 'cranking'). At the front of the floating diver is a vane, the size and angle of which determines the plug's action: large and low angled vanes cause the float to dive deeply; small but deeply angled vanes work at shallower depths.

BELOW A SELECTION OF PLUGS.

ABOVE A SELECTION OF SPOONS.

As their name suggests, sinking divers sink when cast into a river and allow the angler to explore different depths using the same lure while spinners tempt fish through a combination of visual attraction and vibrations caused by revolving metal blades.

Tip
All predatory fish have sharp teeth and can bite through monofilament line very easily, so use a wire spinning trace when lure fishing.

Points to consider when using lures:
• There are an enormous range of lures to suit different situations.
• The angler needs to consider carefully the species of fish being targeted.
• The prey of the targeted species may influence the size and colour of the lure required.
• A lure must be 'given life' by the angler to trigger a response in the fish.
• The lure must be put into the predator's taking zone.
• The tackle that the angler uses will affect the way the lure behaves.
• Sharp hooks are essential.
• Because the lure appeals primarily to the fish's visual sense, water clarity is important; in coloured water though, vibrations are more important.
• Think 'size-colour-action' when deciding whic lure to use.

You've got your tackle and your bait, the next step is to set up your 'fishing station' so that you are comfortable:

• Set up one rod, or pole, and then plumb the depth of the water and mark the depth on your rod (typewriter correction fluid is good for this). Any additional rods or poles can be set up and aligned against this mark.

• Set your keepnet in the water.

• Set up your seat or seat box.

• Get your landing net and accessories together (and anchored down if need be).

• Mix up your groundbait.

• Adjust your bank sticks and rod rests.

• Get your bait ready.

• Cast in, throw in groundbait and wait patiently for a bite.

CASTING

Once you've plumbed your swim so that the groundbait is just touching the bottom, you need to cast to that same spot. Casting accurately is vital: a metre either side may mean that the bait is higher in the water and you could miss a bite. Erratic casting, moving the bait around and 'scattered' loose feeding send fish all over the swim instead of attracting them to one small area. The same is true of feeder fishing: you need to concentrate the bait in a small area of the swim so you need to cast into the same spot every time.

RIGHT THE START OF THE UNDERARM CAST.

The biggest mistake novice anglers make when casting is to cast with the rod out to the side: the best, and most accurate, cast starts with the rod directly over your head pointing straight up into the sky, that way the float, feeder or lead will fly straight out in the same direction every time:

• Select a static point on the far bank – a tree or telephone pole is good.
• Wind the float, feeder or lead to about 90 m (3ft) from the end of the rod.
• Open the bale arm of the reel and trap the line with your forefinger.
• Hold the rod vertically and point the butt of the rod at your marker point and the tip just behind your head.
• Punch the rod and rig out towards the marker and release the line just as the momentum carries the rig to its 'spot'.

All you have to do is to focus on achieving the same distance each time you cast. You can do this accurately using a fixed-spool reel with a clip line:

•Cast to the point you want to fish.
• Tighten the line so there is no slack.
• Wrap the main line around the line clip while the rig is still out there.

You can now recover the line, but the next time you cast out, the line will be released until it reaches the piece looped around the clip. The only drawback with this is that, if you hook a really big fish, it's likely to snap the line because you can't release extra line from the reel, because it's secured by the clip.

The more you practise casting, the better and more accurate you will become: some leisure fisheries have what can be best described as 'casting practice areas' with 'hula-hoops' of different sizes and at different distances from the banks. You can practise casting into the floating hula-hoops to perfect your technique.

STRIKING, PLAYING AND LANDING FISH

When the tip of a float wobbles, then sways and then disappears below the surface, something has taken the bait. Now is the time for the angler to strike. In the excitement, many novices make the mistake of 'yanking' the rod, a reaction that is more or less guaranteed to lose the fish! If a small fish has taken the bait, such an aggressive strike will rip the fish's mouth. If the fish is big and sets off at speed away from you, yanking the rod will probably snap your line.

Instead of 'striking' at the fish, think more of 'lifting' it: this will help to set the hook. If a big fish is racing away, give it plenty of line immediately by backwinding: the lever on reels known as the 'anti-reverse lever', when set in one position, allows you to pay out extra line. (Set in the other position, the

ABOVE THE ANGLER WANDERS ALONG THE BANK, CASTING INTO PROMISING AREAS.

lever switches this off). Set the wheel's clutch lightly so that it releases the line rather than snapping it. In open water, let the fish have its run rather than trying to stop it (but stop it if it's heading for a snag!). After its first run, ease the fish back towards you, keeping a tight line at all times so it cannot free itself from the hook. Play the fish by 'pumping' it to you: raise the tip of the rod under a tight line, without winding, until the rod is vertical or at least level with you, then quickly wind back to the fish so it's ahead of you. If the fish moves to the left, move your rod to the right – and vice versa. When the fish is about 1½ rod lengths from the bank, you must stop winding because it's now ready for netting: most fish let you know they are ready for netting because they come to the top of the water and take a gulp of air. Place the landing net in the water and draw the fish over it.

RIGHT A FISH IS DRAWN TO THE WAITING NET.

LEFT SUDDENLY SEVERAL ANGLERS' RODS BEND AS THE TROUT COME ON THE FEED.

BELOW WATCH THE TIP OF THE LINE CAREFULLY.

BELOW IT IS IMPORTANT TO SAFELY RETURN 'OVER THE LIMIT'
FISH TO THE WATER.

RETURNING A FISH TO WATER

There are many different reasons why a fish is returned to the water: it might be too small (under the legal limit for the species) or there might be strict limits on the number of fish that are allowed to be taken. Conservation of the species is important: there's no future in fishing unless some of them are returned to the water. Safely and correctly returning a fish to water is important: the fish has battled for its life on the hook, using up its energy and oxygen reserves and risks suffocation. Bacterial infection is also a common cause of death and this can occur if the slime that covers the fish gets damaged on landing and from handling. Always wet your hands before handling a fish to reduce such damage. Deep-water fish that are reeled in quickly often don't have time to adjust to the difference in pressure. Just like divers, these fish can get the bends and often won't survive after being returned to the water.

The hooks, especially barbed hooks, injure and maim fish if they sit deep in the throat, the gills or the stomach and many fish die because the hook is not removed properly. Hooks without barbs and hooks with a single point increase the chance of a fish's survival. If you intend to return the fish to the water, remove the hook while the fish is still in the water if at all possible. If the fish is hooked very deep and the hook is difficult to remove without injuring the fish further, it's sometimes better to cut the line at the hook or break off the hook with tongs. Connective tissue will grow round the hook and the fish will suffer less than if you were to try and remove it completely.

When you release a fish back into flowing water, it's vital that you hold its head against the current: keep the fish vertical, and lower it gently so that its tail is in the water and its head just above. Then wait for the fish to flip its tail. When it does this, it is ready for release but keep a watch on it: if the fish turns bottom up, catch it and hold it vertically again. For some fish it can take a few minutes to recover enough to successfully survive.

FLOAT FISHING

There are three ways to float fish on a river: waggler fishing, stick float fishing and pole fishing (this latter technique is described in the section that follows, see page 90). Waggler and stick float fishing both use a running line whereby you pay out line from the reel as the float travels downstream with the river current.

Waggler fishing is a good choice on slow-flowing rivers: the bait is carried slowly and is easily grabbed by the fish. You can fish wagglers high in the water, just touching the bottom or even at over depth, where the bait bounces along the riverbed (but you do risk snagging a line here). Wagglers should be weighted with split shot (see page 56), so that two-thirds of the float ballast is bulked around the base, with more split shot spread out along the whole length of the hook to make for a slow steady fall of bait through the layers of water, and thereby increasing your chances of a bite at different depths. There is a useful technique called 'mending' the line, where you lift the line from the surface of the water every now and then and place it back behind the float. This is done because the upper layers of water travel faster than the deeper layers: if the line on the top level is carried too quickly, it will pull the float through the water quickly, too, and the bait will look unnatural to the fish. On canals, where the fish tend to congregate on the far side of the water, unless you have a really long (and expensive) pole, waggler fishing is your only alternative. Because the canals have shallow ledges or shelves at either side (the deeper boat channel runs down the middle), canal wagglers are quite short with a tapered shape designed to take just a few split shots to take the float downwards.

Stick floats, because they are attached 'top and bottom', give the angler more control and let you tease the fish with the bait: you can slow down or speed up the progress of the float through the swim, although this can only really be done at short distances from the bank. Stick floats also have a greater tendency to tangle when cast than in waggler fishing: casting here is best done 'underarm' and checking the line by lightly dabbing your finger on the reel's spool so that the rig straightens out as it touches the water and doesn't land in it in a tangled heap!

RIGHT FREE OFFERINGS SUCH AS THIS SWEETCORN CAN BE INTRODUCED WITH A CATAPULT.

BELOW THE ANGLER'S ARM RESTS UPON THE ROD IN READINESS FOR THE DISAPPEARANCE OF THE FLOAT.

ABOVE Accurate introduction of free
offerings will pay dividends.

Float fishing on still water is slightly different: on a river, the current will pull the float under, but on a still lake it will be a fish that does this. This means the fish has a slightly longer time to feel any resistance and drop the bait. Therefore, the float has to be set with just the very tip visible above the surface of the water. Still-water fish won't be expecting bait that moves once it's near the bottom – that would look completely out of place! So, if you're fishing in windy weather, cast a little further out from the spot you want to fish; dip the rod tip under the water and wind in the line by a couple of turns. The link will have sunk and, with luck, any problem with the float moving around too much is sorted. Not all bites will pull a waggler under: sometimes a fish picks up the bait and moves to higher water, thereby raising the lower shot and you'll see the float rise in the water. This is called a 'lift bite', but you would strike as you would for any other bite.

ABOVE ANGLERS WAIT PATIENTLY.

ABOVE SUNNY SUMMER REFLECTIONS UPON CALM WATERS.

POLE FISHING

Pole fishing offers anglers many advantages over stick float and waggler fishing, because it is very accurate and presents the bait very well. With a pole it's very easy to plumb the depth of your swim so the end of a maggot is just tripping the bottom. And, because the top layer of a river flows faster than the deeper layers (which can drag the bait along the bottom in waggler fishing), with a pole you can hold the float back and edge it through the water quite slowly so that it mimics the behaviour of bait more accurately. You need quite a lot of line between the pole tip and the float, which is designed with a 'body-up' shape: the bulk of the shape is towards the bristle at the top of the float. This shape lets the angler hold the float against the flow of the river. The elastic that runs through the top section of the pole also acts as a shock absorber and allows you to use a fine, pre-stretched line without too

ABOVE Dead baiting on a large reservoir in winter.

much fear of it being snapped. Pole elastic comes in various, numbered breaking strains: nos. 3 and 4 are suited to most pole fishing situations but the faster the flow, the deeper the water and the bigger the fish, so the bigger the elastic you'll need.

On canals and still water, pole fishing is even more accurate. In these environments, the fish are most likely to be hiding around and under natural features (reed banks, fallen trees) and the pole lets you push your float right up alongside them. Pole floats for still water have an elongated 'body-down' form while for far-bank pole fishing on the shallow shelves of canals, when you're targeting big fish like carp and tench, you'll need the short float known as a dibber that has a big top for use with large lumps of luncheon meat or paste, where the float being pulled under by the weight.

LEGERING

Legering is an angling technique in which the bait remains stationary on the bed of the river or still water. The bait is anchored with a leger weight or a swimfeeder (see page 15) and the tip of the rod is used as the bite detector: sensitive quiver-tip rods have been specially designed for legering so that when the fish takes the bait and moves off with it, the tip of the rod pulls around or drops back. Quiver-tips come in various strengths – measured in ounces – and you'd probably need a 3-oz tip on a fast-flowing river, while on still water, the finest quiver-tip at 0.5 oz is best.

A very important aspect of legering on rivers is using just enough weight to hold the rig in place against the flow of the water: if, after you've cast into the river, the rig bounces downstream, you need to add weight bit by bit until it stays put. On the other hand, if your rig doesn't move after you cast, it may be too heavy, so remove some weight – again, a little at a time, until you find the optimum weight that just holds the rig in its place.

BELOW MACKEREL MAKE SUPERB DEAD BAITS.

ABOVE SURFACE LURES CREATE A TEMPTING WAKE UPON THE SURFACE. THIS LURE HAS A SMALL PROPELLER AT NOSE AND TAIL.

When you leger on a river, you need to lift as much line off the water as possible or it will be dragged into a large bow and can move the rig out of position: keep the rod's tip high in the air and more often than not, when you get a bite you'll find the quiver-tip indicates this by bouncing backwards towards you.

Most of the time on a river, you'd cast into the middle, but on some venues (or when the river is in flood) you have to fish close in to the bank: link legering is the technique used here. Tie a paternoster link with a four-turn water knot and add two or three size BB split shots to the link. Cast the rig out in front of you and let the river flow bring it into the bank downstream of where you are. You can catch fish from here with your rod held low to the water.

When you leger on still water you need to sink as much of the line as you can and keep a tight line to the rig at all times so that the wind doesn't interfere with it. Keep the rod low to the water: the tip of the rod ideally needs to be no more than 5cm (2in) from the surface of the water. (Although this does make detecting a bite a bit more difficult, you can overcome this by using a target board to help detect movement.)

Groundbait or open-end swimfeeders (which can be used on rivers) are suited to still waters where the fish root around the bottom for food. Fill the feeder and cast it out: as it nears the bottom, the groundbait breaks free and creates a tasty cloud of particles around the hook bait. Accurate casting is key with a swimfeeder, because you want to concentrate the feed in the same area of the swim each time to keep the fish 'corralled'. Use the line clip on the reel and follow the tips in the section on casting (see page 81). Fish can become suspicious of feeders on some waters, so it's worth trying an ordinary lead weight to fool them!

BELOW THE CRAZY CRAWLER SURFACE LURE IN ACTION.

DEAD BAITING

Dead baiting is the technique used when targeting predatory species like pike and perch. Pike seem to like oily dead bait like mackerel, herring and sardines, but perch prefer their natural freshwater coarse fish as dead bait – roach, bream and rudd, for example. Catfish on the other hand are scavengers and generally eat almost anything! Remember that these predatory fish have sharp teeth so you'll need to use a wire trace when fishing: these are available 'ready-made' with treble hooks or with a single large hook. There are three ways to fish with dead bait: legered on the bottom, float-fished or using a 'sink and draw' style. This can work well in clear water where the fish can see the bait clearly, and involves casting out the dead bait and then drawing it back towards you with 'jerky' movements that mimic the action of an injured fish. Consequently, the dead bait needs to be attached to the hook whole and upside down, so that the dead bait appears to be 'swimming' towards you as you draw in the line. On coloured water, smelly and oily dead bait fished on the bottom is the best method; the oil oozes out and attracts the fish. Once again, you need to 'work' the lure to mimic the actions of a dying fish.

ABOVE POLLOCK ARE OFTEN TEMPTED USING LURES. NOTE THE LARGE EYES TYPICAL OF A NIGHT-FEEDING PREDATOR.

LURE FISHING

When you lure fish you need carefully to consider a number of influencing factors:
• Water clarity: with a lure the fish need to be able to see it, so clear water is vital.
• Light: On dull or overcast days you need a bright lure – fluorescent colours like orange, green and yellow. On bright days, shiny silver or copper lures reflect the light best.
• Times: At most venues, predators have pretty fixed feeding times. First and last light are the norm, but some predators will also feed in the day for a hour or so. Take a note of successful catch times and plan your next session accordingly.
• Season: Generally, predatory fish will be more active hunters in the summer, while in winter they are more likely to have followed their prey into deeper and warmer water, so you'll need to fish accordingly.

Understanding a little about the coarse fish species you are targeting is vital: each fish has its own pattern of behaviour, such as different feeding times, preferred baits, and favourite flavour. Armed with a little knowledge about the fish you will be able to land more of them.

BARBEL (*BARBUS BARBUS*)

The barbel is considered one of the hardest-fighting fish: they grow big and strong and can live for between 10 to 15 years. Streamlined in shape with brown flanks and a rounded snout, the most significant features of the barbel's appearance are the four large barbules protruding from its upper lip. The barbel's preferred habitat is a swift-flowing and well-oxygenated river with a nice firm bottom. It likes to feed as darkness approaches: in summer, when it eats voraciously, it likes large chunks of bait, such as luncheon meat, and bunches of sweetcorn; but in winter, it prefers smaller bait like maggots. In heavily coloured water, where visibility is obscured, the barbel can be tempted with a large, smelly bait, such as a bunch of lobworms or some cheese paste.

BELOW THE BARBEL IS A POWERFUL FISH FOUND IN THE MID TO LOWER REACHES OF SOME LARGE RIVERS.

BREAM (*ABRAMIS BRAMA*)

The bream is quite a lazy bottom-feeder fish: its down-turned mouth is perfectly designed for rooting around silt. Humped back with a forked tail, small breams are called 'skimmers' and are silver in colour until they grow to about 450g (1lb) in weight, after which they take on a darker, more bronze colour (the hump becomes more pronounced too). Bream also has very slimy flanks. It can live for between 15 and 20 years. Bream is a shoal fish – if you catch one it's a sure sign that others are close by. When you hook one, move it away from the shoal quickly so that the rest don't get alarmed and flee the area. Bream don't care to chase their food, so a groundbait swimfeeder is the ideal method of fishing for this species: bream seem to enjoy a groundbait made of 50–50 brown breadcrumbs with some chopped up worms (and a few casters for good measure) and a hook baited with a tasty red worms, topped by a caster or maggot.

ABOVE A BREAM ON THE LINE.

ABOVE A FINE CHUB FROM THE LOWER REACHES.

CHUB (*LEUCISCUS CEPAHLUS*)

One of the greediest river fish, the chub has a huge mouth (it will eat almost anything too) and has brassy flanks with large scales and convex dorsal and anal fins. The chub – a member of the carp family – has a powerful set of teeth at the rear of its throat so keep your fingers well clear and make use of a disgorger to remove the hook. Although it thrives in still water, the chub is most often found in the steady flow of the upper and middle reaches of a river but can be seen in clear, fast-flowing shallows picking off food. The chub is a very wary fish: accidentally cast a shadow over the water and it will disappear. Consequently the most favoured fishing condition is when the river is carrying colour, legering with nice, big (about the size of a walnut), smelly (try cheese and lobworm) bait on a strong line (about 2.72kg/6lb) and a size 8–10 forged specimen hook.

LEFT A FINE COMMON CARP IN EXCESS OF TWENTY POUNDS.

CARP (*CYRPINUS CARPIO*)

The Romans introduced the carp to western Europe in the 4th century, after which it quickly spawned and spread through rivers and lakes. It wasn't until the 15th century, however, that carp were introduced to Britain and, today, they are among the most popular species for coarse fishing in still waters, canals and slow-running rivers. Once introduced into a new venue, the wild carp quickly dominated, but cross-breeding now means the chances of hooking a wild carp are slim. Instead, common, mirror, leather, and ghosties are just a few of the dominant varieties. A voracious predator, the carp can increase its weight by about 1.4kg (3lbs) each year and can have a life span of over 40 years. A hard-fighting line snapper, the carp has a long dorsal fin and two distinctive barbules at the corners of its mouth. Fishing is at its best in summer when the fish are most active and, because it will eat anything when hungry, most baits are suitable.

DACE (*LEUCISCUS LEUCISCUS*)

Small and streamlined, with a pointed head, small mouth and bright yellow eyes, silver flanks and a deeply forked tail, the dace is a river fish that can be seen darting through the fast flowing upper layers of water. It likes clear, clean and highly oxygenated water, where it will happily live for 10 to 12 years. Because it likes clear water, it pays to remember that if you can see the fish, they can see you too! Look for them in weir pools and river confluences or a swim where a deep hole starts to shallow off: that's where the dace will be, because the food will have naturally accumulated at the bottom. The dace is a fast-biting fish and quick to drop a bait if it feels the slightest resistance: stick float fishing is the best method with a float attached top and bottom, with maggots as hook bait

and loose feed – little and often to get the fish feeding and hopefully, to bite at the hooked bait by mistake!

PIKE (*ESOX LUCIUS*)

Sleek and powerful, with a flattened head and large jaws, the pike is a big-time predatory fish that lives up to 25 years, and can grow to weights in excess of 18kg (40lb). It leads quite a solitary life and hides patiently in snags, lunging at unsuspecting fish as they pass by. Prey fish are taken 'side on' and once locked in the pike's jaws have no chance of escape, for inside the pike's mouth are rows of tiny backward facing teeth. The dorsal and anal fins are set far back towards the pike's tail, allowing it to propel itself forwards at great speed. Young 'jack' pike weigh around 4.5kg (10lb) and can be very agile, but the biggest pike (all of them female) can be so big that it becomes hard for them to 'lunge' at live

BELOW   A GREAT PIKE CATCH.

prey and consequently they take to scavenging for dead or dying fish – useful for keeping a fishery healthy. Dead baiting on size 4–10 treble hooks is best for catching large specimens but the most important thing to remember is that a wire trace is needed, as a pike will cut through ordinary monofilament or braid line with its teeth. The main line – and rod – need to be strong, too.

PERCH (*PERCA FLUVIATILIS*)

The perch can be found in clean reservoirs, canals, pits and in slow-flowing rivers, where it can live for around 12 years. Easy to identify, it has large and erect spiny dorsal fins, a dark vertical body stripe and red lower fins. An aggressive predatory fish, it's often the first fish caught by the beginner – perhaps because they are not the best fighters. The perch tends to peck at the tails of its prey until it is no longer able to swim and then it closes in. Consequently, spinning in clear water venues can be good, especially if there is a tag of feathers to attract the perch (they feel like the tail of a small fish). The perch also has a taste for lobworms: try fishing on a size 8 hook with a BB size shot 5–7.5cm (2–3in) from the hook. The worm is, in fact, injected with a little air that pops it up off the bottom and makes it wiggle – to the delight of the perch.

ROACH (*RUTILUS RUTILUS*)

[istock] The roach is also called the redfin on account of its red-orange fins, which stand out against its bright silver flanks. It has red eyes and a slightly protruding upper lip. It can be found in most stretches of river and in lakes and canals, and can live for up to 15 years. A small roach will grab at most bait, but once it reaches about 227g (8oz) in weight, it will have 'matured' into a much more cautious fish and will be very wary of any suspicious looking bait. It is nonetheless fast-biting, so float fishing with a stick or waggler and a pole can be the best method. The roach loves bronze maggots – some say they are even tastier with a sprinkling of ground turmeric!

RIGHT ROACH.

RUDD (*SCARDINIUS ERYTHROPTHALMUS*)

Found in shallow and reedy areas of lakes, lochs and slow-moving rivers, there's no denying that the rudd is a very 'pretty' fish with its golden flanks and bright red fins, yet it also looks a bit sulky because its lower lip protrudes! The protruding lower lip signifies that the rudd is a top feeder, picking insects from the water's surface, and consequently for the coarse angler, fishing with a waggler float fixed at the bottom end only (as it allows you to sink as much of the line as possible between the rod and the float, eliminating any surface drift) is the preferred method. Maggots or casters dropped into the swim and a maggot on the hook should encourage a rudd to bite. Even better is to try float-fishing maggots on the hook: place a few maggots in a container with about 6mm (¼in) of water in the bottom of a bait box with a hole cut in the lid. To avoid drowning, the maggots absorb air, which makes them float. This counters the weight of the float and the maggots either sit on the surface of the water or very slowly sink. In either case, they seem to be irresistible to the rudd.

LEFT RUDD.

TENCH (*TINCA TINCA*)

With its green flanks with tiny scales, red eyes, large paddle-shaped fins and two barbules on its upper lip, the tench is among the most hardy of fishes, living in poorly oxygenated water. The tench is also covered in a really thick slime. The tench can be found in gravel pits, lakes, canals and slow-flowing rivers, where they live to about 20 years old. Like the pike, it's the female tench that makes the biggest fish, weighing up to 5.4kg (12lb). Essentially it is a bottom feeders, so it's not too hard to work out where your hook bait should be placed. To make it even easier, the tench gives away its location by sending up a stream of tiny bubbles as it feeds. It particularly likes to hang around lily pads and reed beds, where it can weave around safely out of sight of predators and it is known to feed quite aggressively in the early morning hours – although it can be quite dormant in winter. Float fishing is the preferred method for fishing for tench: when it bites, the tench has a tendency to move off to higher water, so try the lift method described in the section on float fishing (see page 87). Not particularly fussy, a tench will take baits of bread, worms, sweetcorn and maggots.

RIGHT Tench.

FLY-FISHING

INTRODUCTION

Fly-fishing is the art of persuading a trout or salmon – and increasingly today, sea fish – to take an artificial fly made of feathers, tinsel, and even fur, that has been designed to replicate that fish's natural bait. Fly-fishing has a long history – no doubt the first attempts to lure fish with a hook made of bone and feathers were made by primitive man: the use of the fly-rod was well known in Macedonia in the 1st century and was described by Claudius Aelianus who wrote that anglers used red wool wound around their hooks to which was tied two small, dark coloured feathers taken from beneath a cock's wattle.

In the 15th century, *The Book of St. Albans*, was compiled by Dame Juliana Berners, a prioress of the nunnery of Sopwell in Hertfordshire. The 1496 edition, printed by Wynkkyn de Worde, contained treatises on hunting, hawking and heraldry as well as one on 'fyshinge with an angle'. In this, Dame Juliana described using artificial flies on her local river, the River Ver.

Some 150 years later, Izaak Walton described trout fishing on the nearby River Lea in London in his book *The Compleat Angler* first published in 1653. Walton's work was 'continued' by Charles Cotton who added to *The Compleat Angler* in 1676 and describes fishing on the River Dove (dividing Derbyshire and Staffordshire) with instructions for fishing 'fine and far off' for trout and grayling and with much fuller directions for making artificial flies than had appeared in Walton's original text. With this, modern fly-fishing was born.

TOP LEFT STILL WATER TROUT FISHING IS VERY POPULAR.

BOTTOM LEFT A FLY-FISHERMAN AND TRANQUIL WATERS.

PREVIOUS PAGE CASTING A FLY IS VERY REWARDING.

Writers such as F. M. Halford elevated the art of chalk stream dry fly-fishing to cult status in the late 19th century, but these were later challenged by G.E.M. Skues who recognised that trout did in fact take more of their food from below the surface of the water than from the top. The art of upstream nymph fishing was born and developed further by Frank Sawyer who introduced patterns such as the famous 'pheasant tail nymph' and the technique known as the 'induced take'. In the mid-20th century, when a number of reservoirs were opened in the south of England, still-water trout fishing became widely popular, and this branch of the sport has produced a number of innovative patterns and methods. Fly-fishing, which had previously been restricted to stretches of streams or rivers accessible only to their owners or the wealthy, was now open to all: small lakes and gravel pits were netted to remove coarse fish and then stocked with trout and many small, commercial still-water trout fisheries opened to meet the demand for large specimen fish.

While fly-fishing can be pursued as an art, the basic techniques and tactics are no more difficult to learn than for any other angling method. To fly-fish successfully you don't have to be particularly talented, but you do need to have a genuine interest in nature, which is at the heart of all fishing.

Success in fly-fishing requires a watchful eye, sound interpretation of observations made and applying the appropriate tactics and techniques to the fishing situation: the different venues for fly-fishing – streams and small rivers, large rivers or bodies of still water – will impact directly on these.

RIVERS

Many fly-fishermen consider rivers to offer the only true conditions for fly-fishing. There are two main categories, or types, of river – freestone and chalk streams. Each has particular characteristics that affect fly-fishing.

freestone rivers

Freestone rivers are home to salmon, sea trout and small brown trout. These are wild rivers with rapids, shallows, pools and pockets that are fed by rainwater and snowmelt. In general, the fish in these rivers are left to breed naturally, although some may be stocked and controlled at the start of the season by angling clubs. Wet fly-fishing (see page 150) is the technique to use on these waters, where the fish may be much more suspicious than those on chalk streams, preferring to wait until dusk to feast on up-winged flies such as the autumn dun (*Ecdyonurus dispar*) and March brown (*Rhithrogenia germainca*).

chalk streams

Chalk streams are the traditional home of the brown trout but, increasingly, many chalk streams have also been stocked with rainbow trout. Chalk streams are spring-fed by water that has slowly percolated through the limestone hills. They rarely colour up, and so maintain their clarity and flow throughout the year. The alkaline nature of the water encourages a range of insects, in particular up-winged flies, on which modern river dry-fly-fishing is based. The most famous insect here is the mayfly (*Emphemera danica*). For two weeks in May – known as 'Duffer's fortnight' – the trout have an abundant supply of tasty treats and are less cautious in their habits – which is good for the fly-fisherman. After two weeks gorging on mayflies however, the trout are sated and become more difficult to catch. In addition to the mayfly, blue-winged olive flies (*Ephemerella ignita*), large dark olive flies (*Baetis rhodani*), small dark olive flies (*Baetis scambus*), iron blue dun (*Baetis niger*) and pale watery flies (*Baetias fuscatus*) are other important up-winged flies on chalk streams.

The first couple of weeks of chalk-stream fishing are generally upstream dry-fly-fishing only, but from June onwards, nymph fishing becomes permitted. As the autumn approaches, fly-fishermen switch from trout to targeting grayling.

LEFT FLY FISHING IN SALTWATER TAKES THE TROUT ANGLER INTO A NEW ENVIRONMENT.

RESERVOIRS

Since the 1960s, many reservoirs have been stocked with rainbow and brown trout, making fly-fishing a more accessible sport with many anglers wishing to develop tactics and flies specially designed for these waters both on the banks and on boats. Because many of the reservoirs were built on upland areas in regions where there was plenty of rain, some water was either too acidic or lacking in food for trout naturally to increase their weight significantly and so they have to be regularly stocked through the season. In other reservoirs, where trout can feed on sticklebacks and minnows, the trout become more naturalised. Dry flies that represent 'terrestial' insects such as beetles, ants and crane flies are needed to bring the trout up to the surface.

NATURAL LAKES

Natural lakes are stretches of water that formed at the end of the Ice Age and are the natural home of brown trout, salmon and, if there is a sea outlet, sea trout. In alkaline waters, where there is a wealth of insect life, the fish grow big and fat, while in acidic waters they may remain quite small even at advanced ages. Some trout turn predatory, however, (known as ferox trout) and can grow to weigh up to 9kg (20lb).

SMALL STILL WATERS

To find natural trout lakes in Britain you'll have to travel to the Lake District, to Scotland and to Wales. Both Eire and Northern Ireland have a number of natural loughs that are popular destinations for the fly-fisherman. To cater for the growing popularity of the sport, all types of still waters have been stocked: the finest are clear-water fisheries fed by a natural spring or a small river that helps to keep the water temperature down and the oxygen levels up, especially in warm weather. Once water temperature reaches 20°C (68°F), trout become lethargic and stop feeding.

SALTWATER FLY-FISHING

The pursuit of saltwater game fish using fly tackle has increased in popularity in recent years: pioneered in the United States it is now practised worldwide with shark and sailfish, bonefish and tarpon, striped marlin and striped bass fished on the fly. This has given rise to the design of new, specialised gear: 2.7m (9ft) fast-action rods, reels with centre disc drags to slow down fast-running game fish, extra-strong hooks and, of course, specialist flies designed to imitate fish, shrimps and crabs. Once restricted to warm and tropical waters, saltwater fly-fishing is increasing in popularity in the colder water regions of Europe where mullet, bass and pollack are targeted.

RIGHT THIS CARP WAS TAKEN ON A FLOATING DOG BISCUIT IMITATION.

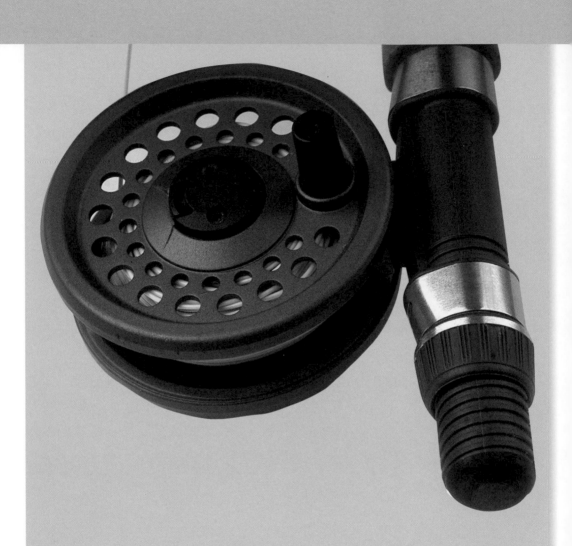

ABOVE THE REEL SITS NEAR THE BOTTOM OF
THE BUTT OF MOST FLY RODS.

RODS

Surprisingly, fly rods have not changed as much in their design as coarse fishing rods over the centuries: Dame Juliana and Izaak Walton would both be able to pick up a modern fly rod and fish successfully with it. The only real difference they would notice is that of the rod's weight: old rods, traditionally made of split cane or greenheart, rods would have been significantly heavier than modern carbon rods weighing just a few ounces.

The role of the fly rod is the same as it has ever been – to cast the fly line – and while it needs to be flexible along its entire length, modern rods have varied degrees of action that are suited to different casting and fishing styles. Fly rods can be categorised by their action and this can be 'fast', 'slow' or 'middle to tip'.

Fast-action rods are light and stiff with the casting action taking place in the top joint. These rods were popularised first in the United States and are used for long-range fishing. Traditionalists tend to prefer the slow action of cane rods, used for river dry-fly-fishing or nymph fishing or in loch-style fishing at short range. They are also used for roll casting and for working flies close to a boat but because they are very flexible,; in a strong wind, these rods can be difficult to hold still. The majority of fly-fishing rods are middle-to-tip rods, where the rod bends under the load of the line from halfway down the blank.

For a fly rod to cast to its full potential, each must be matched to the correct fly line: too light a line, and there won't be enough weight to load the rod; too heavy, and it will overload the rod. In either case, casting distances will be seriously impaired. Each fly rod has an official AFTM (Association of Fishing Tackle Manufacturers) line weight stencilled onto its butt joint: the numbers describe the weight of the line to be used with the rod (this is calculated according to the grains along the first 9m (30ft) of line. Some manufacturers state the AFTM number in a range (for example 7–9) while others are more specific, with a single number indicator.

Fly rods used on rivers are quite short – in general from 1.8–2.6m (6–8ft 6in) and have AFTM line ratings between 2 and 6. Still-water fly rods are a bit longer, ranging from 2.7–3m (9–10ft) long with AFTM line ratings from 6–10. Boat fishing fly rods are longer still: while 3m (10ft) rods are the most popular, rods of 3.5m (11ft 6in) are available for loch-style fishing. A lure rod might have an AFTM rating of 9, while a rod for dry fly may be 6.

RIGHT FLY-FISHING KIT.

NEXT PAGE THERE ARE MANY LURES AND TYPES OF FLY TO CHOOSE FROM.

REELS

Like fly rods, fly reels have changed little over time, as most still operate on a centre-pin principle. The main differences are in the materials used in their construction and the use of high-performance drag systems. Nonetheless, old and especially antique reels by makers such as Hardy, Farlow and Allcock are very desirable collector's items and fetch incredible prices at auction.

The fly reel is basically a storeroom for the fly line, which is stripped off by hand for casting. A fish is then played by releasing or retrieving the hand-held line (although many trout anglers play the fish straight off the reel). Basic fly reels rely on a check system, while more expensive versions have a disc brake. Weight of reels is also important: 'ventilated' (holes drilled in the back) aluminium reels are popular because of their light weight but their shape can become distorted if they get knocked about or dropped and a distorted cage can impede the free turning of the spool.

Because the fly line is weight-matched to the fly rod, so the reel must also match. River reels have a spool of 7cm (2¾in) and carry lines from weight 2 to weight 6. Reels for lakes, large rivers and small still waters have 8.25cm (3¼in) spools and take line weight of size 6–7. Reservoir, sea trout and salmon fishing need much larger capacity spools of 10.2cm (4in) to carry lines from weight 8–12. Many anglers carry a selection of different sized spools loaded with different line that can be quickly changed over if needed. Reels are traditionally set up for left-hand wind, but there are reels available where the configuration can be altered, as some anglers prefer to cast and play the fish with their right arm.

Tip
When you buy a reel, you do need to check that the reel seat will fit on your rod handle, as not all reels are compatible with all rods!

FLY LINES

The fly line supplies the weight that makes it possible to cast tiny, delicate flies. Lines are available in different weights, densities, profiles and colours to match your rod reel and the type of fish you want to catch. The weight of fly line is calculated in grains over the first 9.14m (30ft) of line, and are numbered from 2 (the lightest) to 12 (the heaviest). Lines weighted from 2–5 are generally the best for short casting on rivers, where accuracy is important while heavier lines from 6–9 are suited to still-water fishing, where distance casting with larger flies is needed. Lines weighted from 10–12 are used for salmon fishing and saltwater fly angling where much heavier baits are cast.

If you examine a box of fly line, you'll find information about the profile indicated by pairs of letters. WF stands for Weight Forward: this is the most popular line profile with still-water anglers. Here the weight is concentrated at the front end of the line to allow long casts to be made. DT stands for Double Taper, which is equally tapered at either end, with the weight concentrated in the middle. River fishers often prefer DT line, because it is easy to cast. The line can also be reversed when one end wears out. ST stands for Shooting Taper (sometimes also called shooting head) and is a very heavy front taper that has been spliced to a fine running line of braided nylon to make it suitable for distance casting. To complicate matters a little, the 'weighted belly' part of the line can vary in length from 5.5m (18ft) – the usual length for short casting – to around 9.75m (32ft) for distance casting. Furthermore, you may now find lines marked with the letters TT (triangle taper) and AT (arrowhead taper) to describe the shape of the taper. By looking carefully at the box, you will be able to work out which line is suitable for your use.

Line is also available in different densities and you can select from floating lines, sink-tip, intermediate, slow, medium or fast-sinking line. Many anglers build up a collection of different lines but, to start off with, a floating line is good for use on rivers and lakes, although many still-water anglers find an intermediate sinking line useful, because it allows them to fish their flies just under the surface of the water.

Once fly line was only available in white or ivory – most popular intermediate sinking lines remain colourless – but today, floating fly lines come in a range of colours including fluorescents. Sinking lines tend to be darker in colour. For the beginner, there are handy, budget-priced lines available that have the advantage of coming pre-attached to a braided backing.

LEADERS

In addition to your fly line you'll need a leader – a length of nylon or braid that 'sits' between the fly line and the fly. The leader's length can vary from between 30cm (12in) to more than 6m (20ft), depending on the type of fishing: on still water a leader of up to 7.6m (25ft) might be needed; on a river, a leader of around 2.7m (9ft) is usual, while on reservoirs, a leader of around 4.6m (15ft) is needed. The most important aspect of the leader is that it should taper from the butt section where it is connected to the fly line to the 'tippet', the point where the fly is attached. This taper is what helps the fly to turn over at the end of the cast and land delicately on the water, just as a real fly would. Many anglers still attach nylon leaders to fly lines using a needle knot, by inserting the stiff nylon into the central core of the fly line. Nowadays a braided loop allows you to push the fly line into the hollow end of the braid and secure it in place with 'super glue'. In all cases, think about the breaking strain (bs): for river fishing around 0.9kg (2lb) bs is needed, while on still waters, a minimum of 1.8kg (4lb) is a safe bet.

ACCESSORIES

There are a few fly-fishing accessories that are worthwhile investing in. A pair of sunglasses with polarised lenses not only allows you to see the fish under the surface of the water, but protects your eyes from the sun and glare off the water's surface. If you intend to take your trout home for supper, you'll need a priest – a small cosh for delivering the final blow to the fish's head. If you can, find a priest with a marrow spoon in the handle: you push this down the fish's throat to extract its last meal which could give you an indication of the type of fly you might use to catch other trout. You'll need a pair of sharp scissors for cutting leaders and changing flies, and perhaps a pair of long-nosed forceps for removing a hook from a trout's bony mouth. You'll also need a landing net and, once again, this should be made with a knotless mesh so that any fish are returned to the water unharmed (see also, page 84).

Floatant is needed for dry fly-fishing: this is available in spray form (preferred by river anglers) and in a gel (preferred by still-water fly-fishers. This foam or gel is applied to flies and leaders in order to help them float on the surface of the water. Sinkant, which is a paste that removes grease and slime from the leader, allowing it to cut through the surface film of the water, is also needed in dry fly- or nymph fishing, where you may have to degrease the leader several times during the course of the day.

Fly-fishing (both by tradition and by design) requires the angler to wear a brimmed hat: it shades your eyes and prevents errant flies getting hooked into your hair or scalp. A waistcoat will let you carry everything you need – especially one with expanding pockets. Waders – preferably chest waders – made of neoprene will keep you dry (even if you are just sitting on a wet river bank). Do check the venue, however, as on some still-water areas, chest waders are forbidden and you may need thigh-high waders instead. Whichever you choose, it is worth selecting a pair with strong, rubber soles as these are less slippery on wet grass and muddy banks. On boats, instead of waders you'll need a pair of knee-high rubber boots and, in many instances, commercial fisheries demand that boat anglers wear a life jacket. One of the most popular life jackets is the 'braces' style that slips over the head and automatically inflates if you hit the water.

LEFT CHEST WADERS ARE IDEAL, BUT DO CHECK THEY ARE ALLOWED IN YOUR CHOSEN FISHING SPOT.

LEFT POLARISING GLASSES GIVE VALUABLE PROTECTION FROM THE SUN'S ULTRAVIOLET RAYS.

OPPOSITE THIS HAT GIVES PROTECTION TO THE NECK WHEN FISHING IN TROPICAL SUN.

THE FLIES

Success in fly-fishing is based on the angler's ability to imitate the game fish's natural food. This could include up-winged flies, sedge flies, stoneflies, flat-winged flies, damselflies and 'terrestrial' flies, and even beetles that have been blown onto or into the water from land. Other foods include daphnia (tiny crustacea known as 'water fleas'), freshwater shrimp, water boatmen, water snails, and fry (trout are natural predators and will dine happily on coarse fish fry, such as roach, in the late summer and autumn). For the fly-fisherman, becoming familiar with the particular insect species – their lifecycle and appearance at each stage – is as important as tying flies. There are plenty of books, magazines, Internet sources and fishing clubs that have a wealth of knowledge from experienced anglers who are happy to share tips and information. Fly-tying clubs welcome new members and, because there is always new material appearing on the market, fly-fishermen are keen to discuss the pros and cons as well as to swap patterns. A visit to your local tackle shop will give you a good idea of the vast range of patterns and materials used – and their amazing names: cock cape or hackle feathers; seal and rabbit fur; moleskin and maribou; partridge and golden pheasant, as well as metallic tinsels!

FLY TYPES

The type of fly – or lure – to be used depends on the species of fish being targeted and on the prevailing conditions. Because all flies or lures are designed either to imitate the natural food, or to trigger a response in the fish, anglers must try to imagine what type of lure or fly is needed for a given situation. Using a marrow spoon to reveal a trout's last meal can help: the small spoon is pushed down the throat of a trout and into its stomach, twisted and then withdrawn, with the remains of the last meal evident. If the angler can 'work out' from these half-digested remnants what the trout last ate, he can use a fly that may tempt another trout. As well as being the right size and colour, the fly also needs to be fished at the right depth. Note, however, that a fish will rarely take a fly that perfectly matches the real creature and instead, the angler's fly may exaggerate a natural feature.

THE DRY FLY

Dry flies represent the adult stage of water insects such as olives, mayflies, sedges and midges, as well as various 'terrestrial' insects blown onto the water. Some classic river patterns of flies are over 100 years old and float on the water's surface because of their stiff hackles and tails and whose length is 1½ to 2 times the hook gape. The wings were traditionally tied from matched strips of quill feather, but today a number of other feather materials such as *cul de canard* (literally 'duck's bottom'), the smallest,

fluffiest feathers from a duck's bottom are used, as well as buoyant materials like elk hair and polypropylene foam for keeping the dry fly afloat. Some of the most famous dry-fly patterns in use are the Grey Wulff, Grey Duster and CDC Dun. Spent flies imitate the stage of life when the female flies have completed their egg laying: the female spinners get trapped in the surface film of the water and drift away (to be eaten by trout although a trout can, in truth, be very picky about which spinners it chooses).

THE WET FLY

The wet fly is designed to sink just below the surface of the water and imitate the hatching – or emerging – stage of an insect's life, when it changes from a pupa to an adult. Wet flies can either be hackled or winged and, traditionally, they are fished in teams of three. Famous wet flies are the Mallard and Claret, Greenwell's Glory (which dates from 1854) and Blae and Black (a traditional Scottish pattern that represents the duck fly, a large midge found in Scottish lochs and loughs in Ireland). Wet flies are also used for sea trout in lochs and rivers and famous patterns for these include Wickham's Fancy, the Bloody Butcher and Alexandra.

NYMPHS

It was G.E.M. Skues who developed the art of nymph fishing on the crystal clear chalk streams of southern England. He witnessed the trout as they darted from side to side, taking the nymphs as they swam in the water. He realised that the trout could be tempted on imitations of these when the dry fly failed to work. The term 'nymph' applies to a huge range of flies that imitate aquatic flies in their various stages of life: as well as nymphs, they can imitate a fly's life as a pupa, but are also used to imitate shrimps and water boatmen. Nymphs can be weighted or unweighted depending on the depth at which you are fishing: some have polystyrene heads so that they sit on the surface, almost like a dry fly, while weight can be added in a number of ways including winding lead wire or foil around the hook shank. On the lighter and more delicate river pattern nymphs that are fished just below the surface of the water, copper wire is more often used. There are also gold bead heads, and on rivers where their use is permitted, they not only add weight to nymphs but also add an extra 'flash' to attract trout and grayling. Some of the most famous nymph patterns are Walker's Mayfly (a classic English pattern devised by Richard Walker), Killer Bug (devised by chalk-stream angling legend, Frank Sawyer) and Pheasant Tail. In running water, the nymph should be fished upstream in the same way as a dry fly. In still water you'll need to retrieve the nymph very slowly to make it look realistic.

SALMON AND SEA TROUT FLIES

Although they are fished primarily in rivers, salmon and sea trout can also be fished in certain lochs and lakes. Salmon does not feed in fresh water, which is why its readiness to take a bait or lure is a subject of great debate among anglers. It's not known whether a salmon takes a lure as a reflex instinct from its feeding days at sea, or, as an aggressive reaction to something having invaded its territory. Most flies used for fishing salmon are fished downstream, in the same way that wet flies are fished for trout. In the 19th century, William Blacker, an Irishman who operated a tackle shop in Dean Street, in London's Soho, was regarded as the finest trout and salmon fly dresser of the age. Fortunately, Blacker described and illustrated his dressing methods in his book *The Art of Fly-making* which first appeared in 1842. Two famous salmon flies are the Garry Dog (a Scottish pattern often used on rivers that carry a peat stain) and the Willie Gunn Tube.

RIGHT NYMPH PATTERNS IMITATE THE LARVAL STAGE OF AQUATIC FLIES.

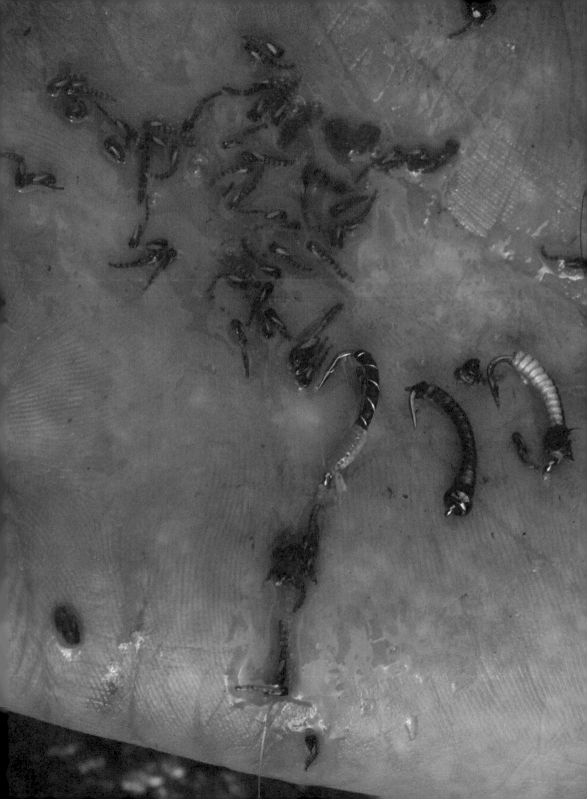

Although sea trout is the same species as brown trout, it has developed the urge to migrate to sea, where it feeds on richer sources of food than those found in the rivers of its birth. Consequently, it grows much bigger than its non-migratory cousins. Like the salmon, the sea trout returns to its home river to reproduce. It can be caught using specially designed flies or 'ordinary' trout flies and is best fished for after dark. In North America, some rainbow trout also develop a migratory strain known as the steelhead, which is fished for using the same techniques as for salmon.

LURES

Lure fishing was developed for fishing on large reservoirs where anglers fished for rainbow trout. Lures are tied to imitation fry or other forms of aquatic life, such as tadpoles. They often bear no resemblance to the actual creature, but are instead designed to imitate their flash, colour and movement. Tiny, soft marabou feathers (taken from the marabou stork) undulate beautifully underwater and are used for the tails and wings of lures although, increasingly, scintillating man-made fibres are being used to add more flash. Lures are fished at a various speeds to provoke trout attack and you'll need to experiment to see what speed is needed in particular circumstances. Be prepared to alter your methods as the day progresses. Some lures have been developed for fishing in specific ways: boobies, for example, are extremely buoyant lures often used in conjunction with a fast-sinking line and a short leader: the line sinks to the bottom, the lure then rises to the surface. Be aware though that on many catch-and-release waters, boobies are not permitted. Some of the most famous lures are the Yellow Booby, the aptly named Appetiser and the Dog Nobbler (later known as the Orange Leadhead).

PIKE FLIES, SEA FLIES AND FLIES FOR COARSE FISH

The pike is a fierce, predatory fish that can provide the fly-fisherman with good sport. The lures that are used to tempt it imitate real fish or water creatures that it is likely to devour. Large flies are created using bright materials that will attract the pike's attention, while other lures are bulky in order to create wake and disturb the water, drawing the pike to them. Remember that if a lure is to resist the pike's rows of razor sharp teeth, a wire trace is essential.

Fly-fishing in the sea is growing in popularity: bass, pollock and mackerel provide excellent summer sport in British waters, while strong, fighting fish such as bonefish, tarpon and sailfish are targeted in warmer climates. Sea flies often have bright, silvery lures in imitation of sand eels, prawn and fry. Tackle needs to be resistant to saltwater corrosion and the flies used in saltwater fishing need to be tied on stainless-steel hooks.

Several species of coarse fish can also be caught on the fly: chub, dace and roach are among those that will readily take small trout flies or nymphs, while carp can be tempted with an artificial floating dog biscuit crafted from cork or deer hair.

LEFT The airborne fly line is the casting weight.

START FISHING

The novice fly-fisherman is best advised to start off with a rod 2.9m (9ft 6in) long, with a number 7–8 medium action. Hold it and see if the handle fits comfortably in your hand: some may feel too thin, others too thick. Modern fly rods are generally well made, but the walls of a glass-fibre blank can be thin and may even shatter if struck by a heavy fly. A reputable tackle shop will spend some time with you and be able to advise you on your purchase.

At first, your reel will only be used for storing your line, but you will need an extra spool to hold an extra line. And when it comes to flies, there are dozens to select from, but a good starting point is to get a floater and a medium sinker with a small mixed box of lures and nymphs from size 12–8. You'll also need some 25m (82ft) spools of leader material in 2.27kg and 3.18kg (5lb and 7lb) – and choose clear line too. Don't forget you'll also need a knot-free landing net. Put on your polarised sunglasses, your hat, your waistcoat and your waders and you're nearly ready to fish.

If your rod is a two-piece model, slide the sections together making sure that the rings are carefully aligned in a straight line. Screw your reel onto the bottom of the handle, making sure the line comes off the top of the reel from the front and not the back, then thread the line reel through the rods rings. When you get to the top ring, pull off several yards of line: if you don't, the weight of the line will pull it back through the rings and you'll have to start the threading all over again. Tie on a leader of 3.7m (12ft) and attach your chosen fly. Now, you are really ready to fish.

1THE ANGLER STARTS WITH THE LINE STRAIGHT
OUT IN FRONT OF HIM.

CASTING

It is important to be able to cast well, and it is a good idea to take some lessons. You can practise further in a quiet field or in your garden (if it's a good size). Instead of a fly, tie a small piece of wool into the leader, making sure there's nothing behind you for it to snag on.

The basic overhead cast involves lifting the line from the water, sweeping it upwards and behind you to load the rod, and then casting it forwards. Ideally you should keep your wrist straight and your arm movement should take place at the elbow: letting your wrist break (bending it at the back-cast moment) will drop the line behind you, most likely snagging on trees or bushes behind you. Use your thumb, upright, to stabilise the rod handle: as the line is lifted from the water, the rod will flex backwards. Don't take it too far back though – try to keep it at the 1 o'clock position and let the tip do the work.

When the line has extended straight out behind you, gently start to bring the rod forwards again: don't cast too early or your action will end up like a whip crack and you risk losing the fly. If you leave it too long, the line will simply lose momentum and drop to the ground behind you.

The aim is to cast a parallel line with small, narrow loops: when the line comes forward aim for about 1m (3ft) above the water to give the loop time to straighten out and extend before dropping in the water. You want the line to land as straight as possible but also with the tiniest splash possible: don't forget your fly is mimicking a real fly landing on the water not a dive bomber!

3 HE ACCELERATES INTO THE BACK CAST, SO FLICKING THE LINE BACK OVER HIS SHOULDER.

7 AT THE SAME MOMENT HE BEGINS THE FORWARD CAST, USING THE LOADED ROD TO PUSH THE LINE FORWARDS.

4 HE PAUSES WITH THE ROD AT '1 O'CLOCK'.

8 THE LINE WILL TRAVEL FORWARDS.

5 THE LOOP OF LINE WILL NOW UNROLL.

9 THE LINE LANDS IN A STRAIGHT LINE IN FRONT OF THE ANGLER.

6 WHEN THE LINE HAS STRAIGHTENED BEHIND HIM, THE ANGLER STARTS TO PULL DOWN WITH THE LINE WITH HIS LEFT HAND.

10 THE ANGLER CAN NOW START TO FISH OUT THE CAST BY RETRIEVING THE FLY OR ALLOWING IT TO DRIFT ACROSS THE FLOW OF THE RIVER.

shooting a line

Once you've got the hang of the overhand cast, you then need to shoot some line to gain extra distance. Pull off some spools of line, keep some spare line in your empty (rod-free) hand and let the spools fall to the ground. Keep the tension on the line, accelerate the rod to the vertical and stop it there: when the line has straightened out behind you, bring it forward, releasing some of the spare line held in your other hand.

You'll also see fly-fishermen moving the rod backwards and forwards between 1.30 and 11 o'clock over their heads several times: this is called false casting and releases more line into the air as the rod is moved forwards and back. This technique increases the speed at which the line travels – and it dries out water-logged flies too!

hauling

This method of casting allows fly-fishermen to cast to great distances, because the technique increases the speed of the line. The hand that is not holding the rod hauls (pulls down on) the line quickly during the lift and releases it during the forward cast. This is known as a single haul, but you can also do a double haul, where the line is pulled twice quickly: once on the lift when the line is released on the back cast, and again on the forward cast. It takes some coordination, but the more you practise, the more fluent you'll become.

roll cast

The roll cast is a method of casting a fly without using a back cast (see above). The line is lifted off the water to the side of the angler and rolled forwards. This technique is used by river fly-fishermen, especially when there are trees or high banks behind them. A roll cast starts with the line under tension on the water with the heavy belly of the line behind the angler: the rod is lifted backwards and upwards in a semicircle to pull the line across the surface of the water. When the line is lopped behind the angler, in a single flowing movement, the rod is brought forwards to roll the line out.

RIGHT ROLL CASTING IS A GOOD TECHNIQUE
NEAR HIGH BANKS.

serpentine cast

A serpentine cast helps in dry fly-fishing to smooth out uneven water current conditions and extend the drift of the fly. When the line is shot out, the tip of the rod is whipped from side to side in short, horizontal lashes. The line follows the movement and falls in curves on the water. If the middle current in the water is the strongest current, it will take up the curves in the line before it can take hold of the fly.

spey cast

The roll cast (see page 146) forms the basis of the spey cast, which is used by salmon fishermen: a single spey is used by wading anglers when a strong wind is blowing upstream; a double spey when it's blowing downstream. In a single spey, the salmon rod is raised and swung around upstream to bring the line and the fly off the water. After lifting, the line has to strike the water to create a big loop, which is used to push the fly back upstream of the rod. The more complicated double spey requires the line to be swung downstream to create a loop.

LEFT CASTING WITH A SPEY FLY ROD.

WET FLY-FISHING

Fishing with wet flies is the oldest form of fly-fishing: before the use of dry flies that float on the surface, wet flies were common. Alfred Ronald's book *Fly-fisher's Entomology*, published in 1836, contains numerous patterns of wet flies, many of them in use today. Since the salmonoids feed predominately on food found under the water's surface, wet fly-fishing can be very effective, and although European and North American fly-fishers now tend to fish with nymphs (see page 156), wet fly-fishing remains a popular choice with British and Irish anglers. River wet flies are fished downstream in Britain and have spidery shoulder hackles. They imitate nymphs, emerging duns and drowning spinners. Winged wet flies (like the Coachman and Butcher) are fished upstream.

In running water, wet flies are used alone, either just below the water's surface or deep down. In the classic manner, they are cast across the stream or river and fished downstream. It is important that the fly is allowed to follow the stream and then, at the end of the drift, brought gently back. Each cast should be 'fished out' completely as it is often during the very end phase of the cast that the fish takes the fly. In shallow water, a floating line works well, while in deeper water, a sink tip or sinking line is better suited. A rod with a good action about 2.5–3m (8–10ft) long and a line number 5–6 would be good for guiding the fly and handling the line.

In still waters, the fly is presented with active movements: after the cast they are moved very slowly, with some small 'jerking' motions. To fish deeper pools, a sinking line is used as well. On large, open surfaces of water a longer rod – about 2.7m (9ft) – is used. Flies that are fished near the surface allow the angler to see the fish breaking the surface of the water: when the swell becomes apparent, the time has come to set the hook by carefully, but firmly, lifting the tip of the rod and stretching the line at the same time. In deeper waters, a nibble might feel like a small tug or a definite jerk, and the fish can be hooked in the same way. In downstream fishing, however, the fish will often hook itself, but if you miss your fish, move upstream, paying attention to the water under the banks, around large boulders and fallen trees, and try some of the larger eddies or where the current narrows.

RIGHT IN RUNNING WATER, A WET FLY WOULD BE USED ALONE.

TOP LEFT WET YOUR HANDS BEFORE HANDLING THE FISH.

BOTTOM LEFT DRY FLY HAS TEMPTED THIS SMALL TROUT.

DRY FLY-FISHING

Perhaps the main reason for the popularity of dry fly-fishing is that everything happens in the open and can be seen by the angler. Dry fly 'fever' broke out in Britain in the 19th century on the chalk streams of Hampshire. The method was described by George Pullman, in 1841, in his book *Vade Mecum of Fly-fishing for Trout* while dry flies of the day were popularised through books such as F. M. Halford's *Floating Flies and How to Dress Them* of 1886. Owing to the different landscapes, and consequently, different kinds of fish and insects, new patterns and styles of dry flies have emerged over the past 100 years or so. But the general principle of dry fly-fishing remains the same: fish that rise up to drifting insects on the surface of the water can be tempted with artificial flies.

Ideal dry fly-fishing times are, therefore, when the fish are active near the water's surface. However, even when there are no tell-tale rings on the surface of the water to indicate a fish's presence just below, dry fly anglers will seek out 'tried and tested' spots using a floating line and long leader. Trout don't rise vertically in the water, but instead drift back on the current to intercept the fly before returning to a favourite spot in the stream (usually between weed beds, in a shallow gravel run, under a bridge or overhanging tree) waiting for the next meal. In addition to the classic rise (where a series of concentric rings radiate outwards on the water's surface as the trout takes a fly), there is the nebbing rise (when a trout pushes its nose right out of the water as heavy hatches of flies hover above its head); the splashy rise (energetic splashing that usually happens in the evening when trout are after mayfly or caddis); the sipping rise (when insects are trapped in the surface film, the trout usually leaves behind a small bubble); the sub-surface rise (here the trout appears to be rising to the surface but is actually taking an emerging nymph); and the head and tail rise (usually seen in smooth stretches of water, when the whole fish appears as it takes a nymph trapped below the surface). Observing how the fish are rising helps

the dry fly angler to select the appropriate fly and present it in a way that the fish will accept.

In running water, flies are usually presented up or across the stream – the best place to approach a rising fish without being seen. The fly is placed upstream and allowed freely to drift down to the position of the fish: with luck the fish will rise and take the fly. A tug on the line is needed when this happens, because a stretched line is often enough for a diving fish to set the hook firmly. If you are wading, try to place yourself directly downstream of the fish so that when you cast, the fly drifts down over the fish with minimum line drag.

Easter marks the start date of fly-fishing on reservoirs and in the first few weeks the native stock fish generally take any fly that is cast. The resident trout that have over-wintered, however, will be far too clever, demanding flies that are closer to their

BELOW THE CRYSTAL CLEAR WATERS OF THE RIVER TEST IN SOUTHERN ENGLAND. DRY FLY-FISHING DEVELOPED ON ITS HALLOWED BANKS.

natural food. The fish will be concentrated close to the banks in shallow water and the water will be cool, so a sinking line and lure might be the best tactic. As the water warms up in summer and insects like midges start to hatch, the trout turn to these natural foods so the fly-fisher needs to change approach: a floating line with a long leader and a leaded nymph may work here. At this time, too, the fish will feed close to the banks in early morning or evening and move out of range of the angler during the day.

Autumn brings an abundant supply of coarse fish fry for trout to feed on: Minkies (made from a strip of mink or rabbit fur) or a Floating Fry (a pretty accurate representation of fry) are recommended. In winter, when the water levels in reservoirs are generally lower – but the water is very clear – fishing is tough. Rainbow trout will still feed in water down to 5°C (40°F), but a warm spell in the middle of the day may encourage a late hatch of midges to tempt these, and brown trout, to rise. Note that a brown trout caught inadvertently after the end of October must be returned to the water.

LEFT WORKING UPSTREAM, CASTING WITH A DRY FLY.

OPPOSITE THE ARTIFICIAL FLY IS PROBABLY THE MOST ENJOYABLE AND EFFECTIVE METHOD TO USE ON SMALL TROUT STREAMS.

NYMPH FISHING

For each trout that can be seen flying along a river, there are probably ten more hidden away, happily feeding on nymphs and other invertebrates like shrimp and caddis. To tempt these deep-feeding fish, anglers such as G.E.M. Skues and, later, Frank Sawyer introduced new techniques such as the 'induced take', which requires casting far enough ahead of the rising fish that the nymph sinks to its level and can then be pulled up through the water at the last moment by lifting the rod. Hopefully, instinct will encourage the trout to grab at the nymph as it passes by: watch carefully for a flicker of white as the trout opens its mouth, and then strike. It is also possible to 'dead drift' if there is no evidence of fish rising: cast the weighted fly upstream on a shortish leader and allow it to drift back towards you.

BOAT FISHING

Fly-fishing from a boat is popular. For trout fishing, drifting, trolling and anchoring are among the most frequently used styles. Drifting, also known as 'loch-style' fishing because of its Scottish origins, involves a pair of anglers casting and retrieving up to three flies in front of a moving boat. The rules are that you can only cast from the front of the boat, you should not cast in front of other anglers and, where there is a group of boats on the loch or lake, each should drift at the same angle across the waves (usually achieved by starting the drifts well away from each other, and with the boat engines all on the same side, usually the port or left side of the boat. Equally important, at the end of the drift, is not to start the motor up or move across another boat's drift.

When the wind is light, boat anglers fish dry flies and nymphs on floating lines; on windier days, sinking lines are more suitable: finding the depth at which the fish are feeding is all part of the day's angling.

Trolling uses the boat – either by engine or by oar – to move the fly. This allows long lengths of line to be let out so that the fly can be sunk to great depths and, because the boat covers a large area at a pretty constant speed, this method can be extremely good for catching big fish. Popular in Scotland and Ireland, this method for catching stocked rainbow trout is, however, banned on English reservoirs. Two anglers can fish in this way, taking it in turns to cast by letting the fly swing around in an arc behind the boat (known as the 'Northampton style').

Early in the season, on a reservoir, trout tend to shoal up in a bay close to the bank. This is when boat anglers drop anchor and fish a lure (or a boo-bie, where their use is permitted) on a fast sinking line. With the wind behind the boat and no anglers on the bank, you can cast into the bank and, by gradually letting out the anchor rope, can cover a bit more of the water. A pair of anchors – one from the stern of the boat and one from the bow – work even better, as they keep the boat broadside to the bank and stop it from swinging around.

Tip
Always make sure the anchor rope is securely attached to the boat before dropping it overboard!

FLOAT TUBING

Originating in the United States, increasing numbers of British and European still waters allow fishing from float tubes. In their most basic form, these are simply large (truck-sized) inflated tyre inner tubes: now they come customised with canvas covers, webbing seats and storage and floatation

compartments. The angler sits in the tube and propels it by using diving fins (keeping splashing to a minimum), paddling against the wind and treading water to keep the float stationary for casting. The float tube allows you to nymph and dry fly-fish without alarming the fish too much. A short handled net and fly boxes that float are useful accessories. It's good leg exercise, but beware being blown into the middle of a very large expanse of water because you'll have to paddle furiously to get back to the bank. It's also a good idea to wear a life jacket for extra security.

SALTWATER FLY-FISHING

Once restricted to warmer waters of the Florida Keys, the Bahamas and Mexico, saltwater fly-fishing has now spread to Europe, where coldwater species like mullet, bass and pollack are successfully caught. Heavy freshwater tackle can be used, but specialist saltwater gear is also available: long rods, anti-reverse and centre-disc drag reels, stiffer saltwater lines, stronger hooks and flies that don't go floppy in warm waters with temperatures above 20°C (68°F).

LEFT FROM TOP TO BOTTOM THE SKILL OF CASTING LIES IN TIMING AND LOADING THE ROD TO GIVE MAXIMUM PERFORMANCE.

ABOVE WATCHING BAIT SAIL OUT INTO THE
DISTANCE IS VERY REWARDING.

SPECIES

The salmonoid family of fish are desired both for their sport and for their flesh. Although they originate in the northern temperate zones of Europe, Asia and North America, they are now stocked in cool, clear water across the world. The distinguishing features of salmonoids are the small adipose fin situated between the dorsal fin and the caudal (tail) and their spots or parr marks along their sides. As they have been hunted for centuries, ever diminishing stocks have meant that, today, many rainbow trout, salmon and Arctic char are farmed.

RIGHT ADMIRING A FINE ATLANTIC SALMON.

ARCTIC CHAR (*SALVELINUS ALPINUS*)

The Arctic char is a wild relation of the brook trout and inhabits deep, clear glacial lakes where it has been recorded to live at depths of 120m (400ft). With the advent of salmon farming, the size and weight of the Arctic char has increased, as the fish has learned to feed on waste food pellets that escape through the salmon cages. Dark green on its back, with mottled cream markings on its flanks, at spawning time, the Arctic char has a bright red and orange belly and brilliant white leading edges on its belly fins. Not an easy fish to catch on the fly, it prefers calm evenings or night-time to feed on small flies and its season in the UK runs from March to October.

ATLANTIC SALMON (*SALMO SALAR*)

Inhabiting the clean, cold-temperate and arctic rivers of the northern hemisphere, the salmon is the king of fish to many anglers. Bright silver with a few dark spots when run fresh from the sea, as it ripens for spawning in freshwater in late autumn and winter, the salmon turns to a bronze-pink. The cock fish (male) acquires a reddish-brown mottling and a pronounced kype (hooked lower jaw) while the hen (female, known as a kelt) takes on a beautiful purple-coloured sheen. A young salmon returning to freshwater after one winter in the sea is called a grilse and those returning after two or more winters at sea are known as springers. When ready to spawn, the hen fish selects an area of gravel in the feeder streams or headwaters of fast-flowing, cool rivers. There she cuts her redd (nest) into which she releases her eggs that are then fertilised by the cock. The redd is then covered to prevent hungry trout

LEFT SMALL BROWN TROUT PROVIDE EXCITING SPORT.

ABOVE A BEAUTIFUL BROOK TROUT.

feeding on the spawn. Exhausted, the hen fish drops down the river into deeper water to recover before returning to the sea; few cock fish survive beyond this stage. In spring, the salmon eggs hatch into alevin (a stage in which the young feed from an external yolk sac) and remain in the redd for several weeks before they emerge as fry. After two or three years in the river they have grown into smolts measuring 15–20cm (6–8in) long and are ready to drop downstream into saltwater. Once at sea, an abundant food supply brings on rapid growth. Three years later, a salmon responds to the urge to return to its native river to repeat the cycle of life. February to September is the salmon fishing season, but actual start dates vary from river to river.

BROOK TROUT
(SALVELINUS FONITNALIS)

Members of the char family and a native of cold water regions, the brook trout, or 'brookie', is a particularly colourful fish: the back is a greyish-green with very distinctive 'vermiculations' (mottling) that forms a marbled pattern. Cream to greenish-yellow spots along its flanks are mixed with red and blue ones and its white belly is tinged with orange that darkens to almost red at spawning time. The anal, pelvic and pectoral fins are edged with white and are backed by a narrow black strip. Natural to North America, the brook trout has been bred and is now stocked worldwide in cool, clear, clean waters, but it thrives especially in the acidic moorland lakes and reservoirs across the UK and Europe. With a tendency to shoal up and being more aggressive than a rainbow trout, the brookie is easier to catch than the more cautious rainbow and brown trout and will often attack a bright lure – even in the coldest weather, as the season is year round.

WILD BROWN TROUT
(SALMO TRUTTA)

This is the brown trout that kick-started fly-fishing: native to Europe, northwest Asia, less so in north Africa, fertilised eggs were successfully transported around the globe during the 19th century. Eggs from the River Itchen in Hampshire were taken to Tasmania in 1854 and these were later used to stock fast-flowing cool clear rivers in Australia and New Zealand. The practice continued and the brown trout was successfully introduced to southern and eastern Africa, South America and North America where, oddly, this native British fish is known as the 'German brown'. In England, however, the wild brown trout is close to becoming an endangered species: water abstraction and pollution (brown trout need highly oxygenated water to survive) and the mixing of strains with stocked fish are among the causes but hopefully with the assistance of the Wild Trout Society, who are safeguarding the few remaining pockets of genetically pure wild brown trout, their future might be secured. In the early winter, the wild brown trout lays its eggs on a gravel bed of a river (or lake feeder stream), which hatch out about 30 days later as alevins. Once these have used up all the food supply in their external yolk sac, they become fry, and then parr, with their distinctive and characteristic finger markings down their sides. All trout have the genetic potential to migrate to the sea, but at this stage it is impossible to determine which will do so. Much slower growing than the rainbow trout, the brown trout also has no spots on its tail fin. It can also have greatly varied markings, ranging from metallic silver bodies with dark spots, to golden yellow with bright red spots; localised populations have their own distinctive markings.

CULTIVATED BROWN TROUT

Although difficult and expensive to rear, the cultivated brown trout can grow very large and comes in a range of colours and shapes, from the highly marked deep bodied small-water fish to the silver-coloured grown-on reservoir fish. Although it can be stocked on still water of any size, the cultivated brown trout does not breed, but instead lives for many years, often without being caught. In the UK, the season runs from the beginning of April to the end of October and fish can be found in small clear still waters, large gravel pits and lowland reservoirs. Young fish are easiest to catch as they tend to hang around the margins of reservoirs in shoals. As they get older and wiser, and turn to more natural foods, they change shape and colour and the longer they remain uncaught, the more sleek and silver they become. If you are lucky enough to go boat fishing for brown trout on a reservoir, keep an eye open for gravel beds or an underwater raised island – this is where they like to hang out!

GRAYLING (*THYMALLUS THYMALLUS*)

Once regarded as vermin on British trout streams, the grayling is now regarded as fair game in its own right. With large scales arranged in rows, a small adipose fin, an underslung mouth, a big, purple-tinged dorsal fin with dark spots and silver flanks with a gorgeous iridescent lavender or

mauve tinge, the grayling is native to fast-flowing rivers across Britain and northern Europe (except in Ireland), with the larger Arctic grayling also found in Lapland, Northern Canada and Siberia. Technically a game fish, because of its adipose fin, the grayling spawns in spring so, on rivers, it has the same legal protection as other coarse fish; the season in the UK runs from mid-June to mid-March. With a slim muscular body, the grayling favours lying in fast, often shallow waters (with some nearby weed cover for protection) where it congregates in shoals. Fish will rise repeatedly to a dry fly from this location and, because they are often reluctant to move away from their chosen swim, it is often possible for the angler to catch several fish from the same shoal. Larger, more solitary fish are more often found in deeper pools or secluded behind a boulder midstream. At spawning time, the cock grayling wraps its dorsal fin over the back of the hen, stimulating her to drop her eggs onto the gravel bed (in contrast to the trout, which buries its eggs).

RAINBOW TROUT (*ONCHORHYNCHUS MYKISS*)

Native of North American rivers on the west coast from California to Alaska, rainbow trout is easily raised in hatcheries and, because it is very tolerant of a range of water types and temperatures, it can be found stocked in rivers and lakes around the world, although in the UK it is considered purely a still water fish as it is an aggressive feeder that could supplant native brownies. The rainbow trout rarely breeds in the wild (an exception to this is in the River Wye in Derbyshire) and consequently enjoys no closed-season protection, although they can run into spawning condition in early winter. When this happens the cock fish becomes black and unsightly, so most fisheries tend to stock only hen fish or triploid (sexless) rainbows. With its bottle-green back with a purple-pink band dotted with small dark spots running along the side from eye to tail fin, the rainbow trout, when stocked in reservoirs or large gravel pits, changes both its colour and shape as it reverts to more natural foods; much of the spotting

LEFT ADMIRING A FINE RAINBOW TROUT.

disappears and a more silver colour develops. These trout are known as 'residents' or 'over-wintered' fish and are prized for their looks and their fighting ability. Although a greedy fish, the rainbow soon learns which flies to avoid and so the longer it remain uncaught, the more difficult it becomes to catch. On catch-and-release waters, they became extremely varied and only the finest lines and miniscule flies will work.

SEA TROUT (*SALMO TRUTTA*)

The sea trout is a fish of great mystery – and consequently of great allure to the fly-fisherman: one day the pools are empty, the next, they have arrived. Low water levels are not a problem for them either – they simply leap from one pool to the next. Genetically sea and brown trout (see page 163) are the same species, and for the first two or three years of its life, the young sea trout is identical to the brownie. But as they grow from smolt to parr, those destined to become sea trout change colour to silver as they head downstream to the sea in spring. Many of the young fish (called herling) do return to their native river after just a few months, but quickly return to salt water, where the longer they stay, the bigger they grow. The adult fish (kelt) spawns in early winter: the female cuts her redd in the gravel bed of a well-oxygenated feeder stream, the cock fertilises the eggs and the redd is covered by the hen fish to protect it. The kelt then moves downstream to deeper water before returning to the sea. Sea trout newly arrived in a river from the sea have a bar of silver speckled with a few black spots. Young fish can be distinguished from grilse (young salmon) quite easily: the sea trout has a square tail (the salmon's is forked) and its jaw extends behind its eye. The longer it stays in freshwater, the darker it becomes, but a large gravid (pregnant fish) can be difficult to distinguish from a spawning salmon as they are similarly coloured at this time. While herling will attack a fly quite readily, older fish are easily scared by noise and light: a warm, moonless night is often the best time for fishing.

RIGHT A FINE SEA TROUT

SEA FISHING

INTRODUCTION

Saltwater fishing is primarily the pursuit of fish that live within the sea or ocean, but there is also a zone that is part way between fresh and salt water, namely estuaries or water systems on which salt and fresh water mix to form brackish water. The Baltic Sea, for example, contains both fresh and saltwater species of fish with large pike (a freshwater fish) feeding on herrings (a saltwater fish).

A huge number of species can be found in the world's seas and oceans and, here, the fish are truly wild, unmanaged by man and with their lives and feeding patterns governed by the seasons, the weather and biological patterns. Marine degradation is also a serious issue: many of the world's previously rich areas are becoming barren. Sea anglers are increasingly playing their part in monitoring marine conditions – levels of pollution for example – and contest anglers use a 'measure and return' or point system to determine their angling skills with limits on the number of fish or the amount of bait that can be legally removed from the marine environment. Angling clubs and their members have a vital role to play in conservation and the major body in England for this branch of the sport is the National Federation of Sea Anglers (NFSA). Scotland, Wales and Northern Ireland also have their National Federations and these combine into the national organisation of the Sea Angling Liaison Committee (SALC), while the world body governing sea angling, to which the British groups are affiliated, is the Confédération de la Pêche (CIPS).

Apart from mankind, by far the biggest influence on the oceans is that of the tides created by the gravitational forces of the moon and sun: spring tides occur during full and new moons when there is the greatest movement of water. Neap tides are smaller and occur between spring tides. Over a 24 hour period in most parts of the world, there are two high and two low tides and before any angler ventures to the shore or out to sea in a boat, a tide table for the fishing area is required. Landmass can also create tidal surges or even double tides, particularly around headlands, islands and similar natural features.

RIGHT AN APPARENTLY ROCKY BEACH MAY HAVE SAND BELOW THE TIDE LINE.

The seasons affect sea angling to a much greater extent than freshwater fishing: fish travel vast distances through the oceans, migrating like birds as they follow the food and water temperatures that sustain their lives. A fish's life is dominated by the need to feed and the urge to reproduce, and sea anglers need to understand where and when they can intercept the species they are targeting.

Weather patterns influence the presence or absence of fish: for example, an onshore wind is likely to produce fish, because it stirs up the sea, dislodging the marine life that becomes the prey for the fish. For this reason, many sea anglers fish into the wind rather than with the wind behind them. Atmospheric pressure also affects fish behaviour: high pressure produces calm seas that, in turn, produce clear water inshore. This means that the fish only venture inshore in darkness when they feel safe. Low pressure, strong winds and big sea are more likely to produce fish from the shore in daylight. On such days, once holiday-makers have deserted the beaches, sea anglers have the space pretty much to themselves.

Sea angling can be divided into two main groups: shore fishing and boat fishing, both of which contain sub-groups according to the fishing environments.

Fishing from the shore presents the angler with a number of exciting challenges, as well as a range of fishing locations. Beaches vary according to their location and local geographical features, and the tidal flow and prevailing weather conditions also have a considerable influence on them.

ABOVE THE SHORE ANGLER AT SUNSET.   ABOVE   ROCK FISHING IN CALM WATERS

SURF BEACHES

Also known as storm beaches, these are typically broad expanses of sand washed by shallow seas and exposed to prevailing winds. In many parts of the world, the difference between the high- and low-tide marks can be a mile apart. Food creatures like marine worms, sand eels and crabs either move in and out with the tide, or bury themselves under wet sand during low water phases. Flatfish such as dab and flounder happily live in just a few centimetres of water and are, therefore, ideally suited to living on surf beaches. Swimming just beyond the surf's edge, these fish move in and out daily with the tides and are also not particularly sensitive to light or wave activity, although extremely bright sunlight and dead-calm water may deter them. These small fish are the food of larger predatory species, such as the European bass, as well as sharks. Bass are extremely

shy of calm, clear water and daylight, so to fish a surf beach on a perfect summer's day may result in total failure for the angler. At night, however, the same beach may be teeming with fish, even when the water is still and clear, but they still won't come really close to the waters' edge, so casting needs to be quite far to get a bite. The best conditions for fishing on a surf beach are when wind, swells and low light combine to make for brisk wave patterns, plenty of underwater currents and reduced clarity: at this time, the bigger predators move in to hunt for the smaller fish and other marine life that are washed from the sand.

SHELVING BEACHES

These beaches are often made up of shingle and large pebbles and are a halfway zone between the flat sandy surf beach (see above) and the sometimes vertical drops of rocks and cliffs into deep

A ROCKY FORESHORE FULL OF POTENTIAL.

water. Likewise, fish species (and fishing tactics) mirror the halfway conditions. The steeper the angle of the beach, the closer together the high- and low-tide marks become: sometimes less than 22.8m (25yd) of foreshore can be exposed at spring tides. This means that fairly deep water is available, even if the angler is unable to cast long distances. From the fish's perspective, the deep water gives them plenty of space in which to hunt and hide, which is also less affected by calm seas and bright conditions. The result is an environment that fish love and so, in addition to flatfish and other small resident species, steep beaches attract migratory fish like cod and bass.

ROCK FISHING

When sea anglers speak of rock fishing they may be referring to casting from a cliff into the very deep water that runs right up to the rock face below. More often anglers are casting from a rocky platform (like a boulder) not far from the shoreline. Deep water can often be found within a short distance of rocks, and a wide variety of species including cod, bass and wrasse can be caught from natural fishing platforms. Rocks, however, can also be one of the most hazardous places to fish: they are slippery and anglers can be swept away by large waves. Never fish alone, don't fish on dangerous rocks at night, and be aware of the times of tides before venturing out, to avoid getting cut off.

MAN-MADE STRUCTURES

Piers, breakwaters and promenades, as well as bridges and harbour walls offer the sea angler direct access to often very deep water. Fishing from these structures is the ideal way for a novice to become 'hooked' on fishing, especially as they may not have developed the long-distance casting skills that are necessary on the shore. Furthermore, the beginner gets to be close to more experienced anglers and soon learns from watching and speaking to them. There are in fact two types of pier: walled and piled. A solid-walled pier opposes sea and tide and the water is consequently forced to flow along the length of the structure, often creating a strong current as it does so. With a piled or 'stilted' pier, the water flows between the supporting columns and tidal pressure is reduced. Of the two types of pier, it is the piled pier that is easier for novices to fish from and most have a dedicated area for anglers to enjoy their day's – or night's – fishing: the water below pier lights are good areas to fish as many species are attracted to the glow.

In many harbours, waste that has been dumped into the sea acts as an attraction to the fish and encourages them to venture within the angler's range. On a harbour breakwater there could be deep water on one side populated by a dozen species, and a wide expanse of shallow mud flats or sands on the other that only attract fish at high tide.

ESTUARIES

The nature of an estuary is determined by the river that flows into it. Some, like the Thames and Severn estuaries, are giant rivers spilling millions of gallons of fresh water and silt into the inshore sea. These great rivers have created huge areas of salt marsh, sandbanks (which can be dangerous at low tide) and creeks: the Thames estuary, in fact, influences the whole of the north Kent coast and most of the coast of Essex. Estuaries are typically rather muddy environments, created by silt deposited by the river over many years. Where the sea meets fresh water a vast array of fish species can be found, many of which – like the mullet –

LEFT THIS ANGLER FLOAT FISHES FOR MULLET
WHILST A SECOND ROD IS FISHED AT DISTANCE
FOR PLAICE ON THE SEABED.

ABOVE FLOUNDER FISHING IN A SHALLOW ESTUARY.

are able to survive in both fresh and salt water. Flatfish and fish that are tolerant of brackish water can often be found here and in the faster waters of the estuary mouth, bass and mackerel hunt small baitfish. Flounder are estuary fish that can survive in water of low salinity, because they are able to adjust the salt 'tensions' in their blood as they cross between salt and fresh water. Salt and fresh water do not actually 'mix' but, instead, remain in layers so it is technically possible to catch both sea and coarse fish at different depths. Local knowledge of estuaries is vital, not just for locating fish but also for safety reasons. On some estuaries for example, the fish follow one bank as the sea enters the river and then retreat close to the opposite bank when it ebbs. Knowing this, anglers are able to fish throughout the entire range of the tide. In rough weather, estuaries provide anglers with a safe alternative to the open sea.

Before boarding any boat it's vital to ensure that all is safe: the skipper should be fully qualified, licensed and insured. If you are venturing out in your own boat then you must have a detailed knowledge of the region you intend to fish, and an understanding of Admiralty charts and tide tables. You must also have a marine VHF radio (monitored by the coastguard on channel 16), flares and life jackets. If you're a newcomer, don't let this put you off fishing from boats, instead join a small-boat club and learn from experienced members.

BELOW WITH A RUSH OF WHITE WATER
BEHIND THE BOAT WE HEAD FOR THE OFF-
SHORE MARKS.

INSHORE BOAT FISHING

Small boats can fish within a couple of miles of the shoreline. Here, the waters tend to be shallower than they are far out to sea, and the fishing areas more influenced by the landmass. Headlands and estuaries affect the way in which the current flows and, consequently, how food – and fish – is distributed. Most charter boats offer inshore fishing on a 'per rod' basis. Charter boats can generally carry 8 to 12 people: many anglers charter as a group, but many skippers also take in-

dividuals and often have a selection of tackle for hire, as well as providing bait. There is an etiquette to charter boat fishing: because the stern positions are most favoured by anglers, a draw for seats is often arranged to avoid arguments; the wheel house should not be entered without the skipper's permission; and gear has to be stowed so it doesn't interfere with other anglers or the safe operation of the boat.

OFFSHORE BOAT FISHING

To venture further out to sea in the search for the bigger fish species, larger boats are needed to reach the reefs, sandbanks and shipwrecks around which fish thrive. Such areas are like an oasis in a desert, offering shelter and food: in the United States, artificial reefs have been constructed of chained to-gether car tyres. On sandbanks you are most likely to catch flatfish, ray and bass; reefs of rock and weed and wrecks are home to dogfish, coalfish, wrasse, pollack and cod.

BELOW GOOD SPORT CONTINUES THROUGHOUT THE DAY.

ABOVE CASTING A BAITED RIG UP-TIDE.

RODS

Owing to the varied styles of fishing and the differing conditions encountered in sea angling, there is no single rod suitable for all occasions: combination, telescopic and 'ordinary' coarse fishing rods are not suitable for sea angling. Instead there are appropriate rods for each type of sea fishing, designed for use in salt water.

shore and pier rods

For beach casting, rod length is important: 3.7m (12ft) rods are the minimum length used in these situations, because the casting distance is proportional to the rod length and distance is crucial to the shore-fishing success. The rod also needs to handle leads up to 170g (6oz). Beach-casting rods break into two sections by means of a spigot joint: some of theses rods have equal-length sections but others have a tip of about 2.7m (9ft) or more, and a butt of about 0.9m (3ft). Rod dimensions also vary depending on the casting styles required: more powerful rods, designed for pendulum casting (see page 203), tend to have a stiff through-action and a soft tip. On most modern beach casters, coasters (a bit like a clamp device that holds a hosepipe to a tap) are supplied to hold the reel in position and can be adjusted to allow precise reel positioning. Rod rings also differ depending on whether they are used with fixed or multiplier

ABOVE SPURDOG ARE MEMBERS OF THE
SHARK FAMILY.

ABOVE A PAIR OF BEACHCASTING RODS SIT
EXPECTANTLY ON A TRIPOD.

reels. Fixed spool rods are marked FS alongside the model number and have larger rings sited underneath the rod. Multipliers are marked M alongside the model number and have a greater number of smaller rings because the reel is positioned on the top of the rod and they are needed to guide the line along the rod, even when it is bent.

boat rods

At around 2.4m (8ft) boat rods are generally shorter than shore or pier rods: any longer, and they would be difficult to store and handle on most fishing boats. Boat rods are available in specific line classes: 5.5–9.1kg (12–20lb) for light estuary fishing; 11.3–13.6kg (25–30lb) for general bottom fishing and light wrecking; 22.7kg (50lb) for heavier wrecking; and 36.3kg (80lb) for serious shark fishing. Beyond this, boat rod classes go right up to the 60kg (130lb) class.

Fixed-reel seats are essential for boat fishin‚g because powerful fish will dislodge and ruin a weak reel seat. You also need tough rings! Uptide rods are slightly longer than 'normal' boat rods (because the angler has to cast uptide, or away from the boat.) They are based on the same design principles as beach-casting rods but are mostly around the 13.6kg (30lb) class.

REELS

Multiplier reels were originally used for spinning with lures and plugs, but became popular in Britain for shore casting and boat fishing, despite the limitations they imposed on distance casting and their habit of overrunning and tangling monofilament line. Today multipliers specially designed for both beach and boat angling can be found. The reel's gears 'multiply' the spool's revolutions for each turn of the handle: ratios of 4:1 (ie 4 spool revolutions to 1 handle turn) are the most common, but you can get them with a 6:1 ratio for rock fishing and boat uptiding. Multipliers are always used on top of the rod so the angler lays the line onto the spool with his thumb. Two particular sizes of reel are used in shore casting: ABU 6500 is ideal for distance casting over sand using a 6.8kg (15lb) line, while for rock fishing the ABU 7000 with a 13.6kg (30lb) line is recommended.

Boat anglers use multipliers almost exclusively, because they can lift substantial weights easily and today specialist models are available, such as the ABU 7500C, which incorporates high-speed retrieves and line capacities for casting lighter lines. All multipliers have a drag system that allows a pulling fish to take line (which prevents the fish from breaking the line). Shore models generally have a star-shaped knob on the handle, which is turned to tighten or loosen the drag as required – and some of these have pre-set drags which loosen the drag automatically, at the flick of a switch. On bigger, boat reels, there is a more sophisticated lever drag system (the lever is on the side of the reel), while others also have a two-speed retrieve system. In all instances, reel maintenance and tuning is essential for multiplier reels in order to keep their running fast and smooth.

BELOW MULTIPLIER REEL LOADED WITH LINE AND SHOCK LEADER.

Fixed-spool reels for saltwater fishing are often no more than enlarged versions of fixed-spool reels originally designed for freshwater spinning and float fishing (see page 87). Compared to multipliers, fixed-spool reels offer a much more limited casting distance but, on the other hand, this makes them ideal for the beginner, who may be able to cast more modest distances. Where a fixed-spool reel is selected, it should have a coned casting spool so the flow of line is not restricted, and a hardened bale roller to prevent line wear.

LINE

The fishing line is the link between the angler and his bait, which may be over 137m (150yd) away, so it must be reliable. It may be surprising that, in sea fishing, unless you are hauling really big fish out of heavy weeds or doing battle with hunting species like sharks, the lines used do not need extremely high breaking strains (bs). Under normal circumstances lines with a bs of 5.44–8.16kg (12–18lb) are adequate. Fairly light lines make sense, because the lighter the line, the further it can be cast, and in beach fishing, the rods aren't particularly good at generating tension: pulling as hard as you can on a powerful beach caster, the most you will achieve is about 1.36kg (3lb) tension for 91.4m (100yd) of line. Modern lines are now thin and strong and co-polymer lines also have less 'memory' than monofilament lines. Braided lines are popular with boat anglers, as their lack of stretch combined with thinness enhances the feel of bites and sea bed at the same time as combating the effects of tidal flow.

RIGHT THE FIXED-SPOOL REEL NEEDS TO BE LOADED TO WITHIN A SHORT DISTANCE OF THE SPOOL'S LIP.

HOOKS, LEADS AND TERMINAL RIGS

Hook technology means that, today, even the smallest hooks can be ultra strong. Using a small hook allows the angler to catch a more diverse range of fish, while large hooks should be used only when fishing for the biggest game fish species. The variations in the length of hook shanks are probably of more value to the sea angler: long shank hooks are best for worm baits (and are easier to remove from the fish's mouth when you need to return it to the water), while short shank hooks are suited to crab, squid and fish baits. Eyed hooks are also better for sea angling, although stainless-steel patterns should be avoided: if these hooks are left in a lost fish, on the sea bed, or on the beach, they will not rust away and are a potential hazard. Sea-angling hooks that degrade in salt water are the environmental solution. Hook sizes for sea angling start at number 10 (remember the numbers get smaller as the hook size increases). Once number 1 is reached, the sizing is suffixed with /0 added, for example, 10/0 or 12/0. Sizes 4/0 to 1/0 are good for shore fishing for flatfish and small species, while size 1/0 to 6/0 are best for bigger fish like bass.

Sinkers for coastal fishing need to be streamlined so that they fly cleanly through the air and anchor firmly in the sea bed. The tidal nature of the environment governs the weight of sinkers that are most practical: around 113–140g (4–5oz) is suited to most shore casting and rock fishing, while the weight can be up to 907g (2lb) for deep waters and a strong tide when boat fishing. The most popular designs are aerodynamic 'bombs' or impact leads with built-in bait clips. These streamline the hook bait behind the lead and release it on impact with the water.

In deep water, sea anglers use the legering technique for presenting bait on the sea bed: they cast a terminal rig containing lead weights and baited hooks. Terminal rigs can be bought 'ready made' for shore or boat fishing, although they can be 'self made' quite easily using a monofilament paternoster. In this, the main line is attached to the top of a three-way link: the second link is connected to the weight and the third link is connected to the hook. The hook 'snood' – the length of line the hook is attached to – can be increased to alter the 'behaviour' of the bait: long snoods allow big fish to 'engulf' the bait, while short snoods give better bite indication for smaller species of fish.

LEFT A SELECTION OF TERMINAL TACKLE USED FOR MULLET FISHING. LEGER WEIGHTS, LINE FLOATANT, FLOATS, CAGE FEEDERS, HOOKS AND TRACE LINE.

ACCESSORIES

Keeping warm and dry, especially in winter, means that in addition to the usual rod rests and shelters, sea anglers also need to invest in waterproof clothing. Rod rests for sea anglers come in a variety of styles, from the monopod that digs into a sandy or shingle beach to folding aluminium tripods, often with double heads that allow the angler to use two rods at the same time. The 114cm (45in) umbrella remains popular with beach anglers: lightweight and compact it also fits into a rod holdall for carrying. The base can be buried in sand or shingle, or strapped to pier railings or the tackle box. There are also fabric side flaps or wings that attach to the main body of the umbrella using Velcro to increase the area of shelter. Top of the range beach shelters are ideal for extended and night-fishing sessions.

Clothing needs to allow for the fact that the shore angler needs to be mobile. Most opt for a 'bib and braces' and 'top coat' ensemble. Some of these have thermal linings and even in-built flotation devices, which are highly recommended for safety. Waders are popular for shore anglers who fish on surf beaches: chest waders are useful in shallow water but are not ideal on rocks, where sturdy studded boots give a better grip on slippery surfaces.

Night fishing requires some form of lighting and among the most useful are the headlamp – a variation on the miner's safety lamp, because they focus the light for casting and landing fish (and for untangling lines). They can be turned on and off quickly and 'green' rechargeable versions are now available. Bait flasks and cool bags are necessary to keep sea-fishing baits cool (but also to stop them freezing in very cold weather). A really essential item is a cloth – and the more it smells of fish the better! This masks any odours that find their way onto the anglers' hands and are then transferred to the tackle, and which could put fish off.

RIGHT FLOATATION SUITS (LEFT AND RIGHT) OFFER PROTECTION AGAINST THE ELEMENTS AND GIVE A GREATER CHANCE OF RESCUE IF THE ANGLER IS UNFORTUNATE ENOUGH TO BE SWEPT INTO THE SEA. THE CAMOFLAGE JACKET (CENTRE) IS MORE IN KEEPING ON THE BANKS OF LAKES AND RIVERS.

BAIT

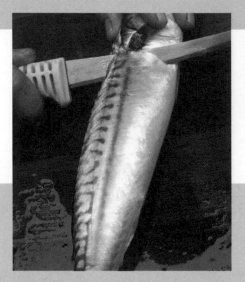

1. A SHARP KNIFE IS ESSENTIAL.

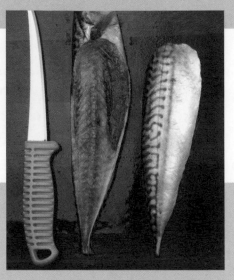

2. One fillet makes a bait for large fish.

3. Cut into strips for smaller bait.

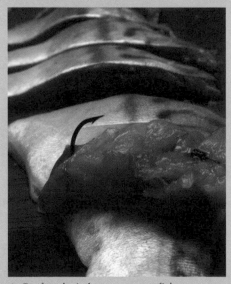

4. Perfect bait for many sea fish.

ABOVE FRESH MACKEREL IS A SUPERB BAIT.

ABOVE THIS POLLOCK HAS TAKEN A WHOLE MACKEREL BAIT INTENDED FOR SHARK.

While some of the baits used in freshwater fishing (see page 69) can also be used in salt water, there is, in general, a greater use of natural baits in sea angling – even if the bait offered seldom reflects the fishes' natural foods! The most important thing about the bait used for sea angling is freshness. Anglers go to great lengths to dig, catch and store their baits: worms are kept in aerated tubs of seawater; fish baits are frozen; and crabs are kept in controlled temperature and humidity.

A basic problem with sea bait is that, no matter how much is placed on a hook, it's always going to look miniscule in comparison to the great expanse of sea. Consequently bait in the sea must attract fish by its smell and appearance.

FISH BAITS

These are among the most widely used baits for sea angling and can be adapted for use in different situations. The big advantage of fish baits is that they can be purchased (or caught), prepared, frozen and stored until needed. Oily fish like mackerel, herring and sardines make superb baits, because of their attractive aroma. They can be cut into sections or strips or fished whole, depending on the size of the fish being targeted. Remember that the size of the hook needs to match the bait and that the bait needs to be placed on the hook in such a way that the target fish is easily hooked. Many small fish can be fished whole as live baits, as the look and smell of the fish and the fact that it emits vibrations as it flutters in the water, make it attractive bait. Predatory species have sensors

ABOVE A SQUID FRESH FROM THE OCEAN.

ABOVE CALAMARI SQUID ARE A POPULAR BAIT.

in their lateral lines that can detect movement at considerable distances.

Sand eel is popular bait that can be bought blast-frozen from tackle shops. These small fish are the staple diet of many birds and sea fish – they are the preferred bait for shore-caught ray in the United Kingdom, and also make superb bait for bass, cod and pollack – although their numbers have been depleted by commercial harvesting as they are also used in fertilisers. The streamlined shape of the sand eel makes it ideal for distance casting, and live sand eels can be collected from sandy beaches after dark. The greater sand eel, or launce, is much bigger. It can also be bought blast-frozen or caught from a boat using special strings of feathered hooks.

Squid is attractive to a number of fish species: calamari can be bought frozen in small boxes and stored until use. When fishing for cod, ray and bass, squid is best used whole on a large hook, or on a pair of hooks known as a 'pennel rig'. Alternatively, squid can be cut up into strips and fished on smaller hooks to attract lesser species; long thin strips can wave about tantalisingly in the tide. Squid also makes a good attractor when it is fished in conjunction with another bait, such as a worm.

All fish bait should be as fresh as possible: the fresher the fish, the firmer the flesh. Decaying squid turns pink, so use your eyes and nose as you would for your own food! Just as you wouldn't re-freeze thawed fish for your own consumption, don't do this with bait: bacteria thrives in this sit-

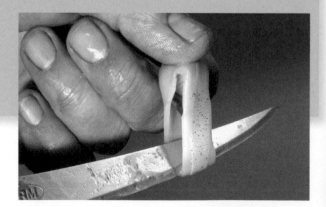

RIGHT SQUID CAN BE CUT INTO SECTIONS, THEN INTO STRIPS FOR USE AS BAIT.

ABOVE LUGWORM

ABOVE TELL-TALE LUGWORM CASTS MAKE LOCATION

ABOVE A FRESH BLOW LUG.

uation, and you can pass on deadly bacterial infections to fish that are returned to the water.

MARINE WORMS

There are many different species of marine worm, most of which end up as food for fish. Anglers should concentrate on worms that are easy to obtain and suitable for impaling on hooks. The hooks need to be thinner, too, and the wire finer than those used for other baits: this will stop the worm from breaking up as it is threaded onto a hook.

Marine worms can be dug from the shoreline or

BELOW DIGGING FOR LUGWORM.

purchased from tackle shops. They need to be stored and transported in a cool container and protected from rainwater and the sun, both of which will quickly kill them. Wrapping worms in layers of newspaper helps to absorb excess moisture. The most popular worm in the United Kingdom is the lugworm, of which there are several varieties. The ones most often used by anglers are the black, or yellow tail, the lug and the blow lug. The black lug can be found well down the beach near to the low-water mark, while the blow lug is found closer to the top of the beach. Once again, you need to be aware of the times of the tides for safe and successful lugworm digging. All lug-

worms leave tell-tail casts in the sand or mud, help-ing the angler to spot them. Be warned, though, that digging lugworms is hard work: a flat-tined fork (the type used for digging potatoes) is the best tool and when you've finished digging, remember to back-fill the holes to preserve the marine environment and ensure that the area is repopulated with lug-worms. Local bylaws may impose restrictions on where worms can be dug, so check first, and never dig for worms close to boat moorings. Lugworms can be used singly, in bunches or as part of a 'seafood cocktail' depending on the species and size of the fish you are targeting.

Ragworms are another family of marine worms of use to the angler, the two most common types being the harbour rag and king rag. The harbour rag is abundant in most estuaries and can be dug up quite easily – remembering to follow safe, good practices. It makes excellent bait for many small species of fish, especially flatfish. Harbour rags are fished in bunches on small, fine wire hooks: thread several worms headfirst so their tails trail attractively in the tide. The king rag is a much larger ragworm that can grow up to a massive 91cm (3ft) long. It attracts a variety of fish species and is generally fished singly, depending on the size of the worm and the fish being targeted.

ABOVE THE PEELER CRAB IS OFTEN PROTECTED BY A LARGER HARDBACK CRAB.

ABOVE PEELER CRABS TEND TO BE LESS AGGRESSIVE THAN HARDBACK CRABS. TREE-

ABOVE MUSSELS ARE EFFECTIVE BAITS, PARTICULARLY WHEN USED WITH OTHER BAITS IN A COCKTAIL.

SHELLFISH

Shellfish are probably only eaten in large numbers by fish following a storm, when the shellfish are dislodged from their anchoring places. Shellfish bait gives off an enticing scent that is highly attractive to many species of fish, especially cod, bass and wrasse.

Mussels and razor fish make excellent baits for many species, either on their own or as part of a seafood cocktail bait. Mussels can be collected from rocks and groynes at low water (or bought from a fishmonger). They need to be carefully removed from their shells with a blunt knife and whipped to the hook using fine elastic. These baits can then be frozen ready prepared on the hook and trace, or wrapped individually in foil, frozen and thawed later for placing on the hook. Razor fish can be collected using a box of salt at low water: sprinkle a little salt over the razor fish burrow and it comes up to your waiting bucket!

The common crab is eaten by many sea fish, as evidenced by the remains found in many fishes' stomachs when they have been cleaned. The best time to use crab is when they are moulting: as crabs grow, they shed their old shells and grow a new one. Before it has shed its shell, the crab is called a peeler crab: the entire outer shell can be removed leaving a soft, jelly like interior that can be mounted on hooks whole or cut into sections. Don't disregard a crab's legs: these are excellent bait for small fish or can be mixed into a cocktail for larger species. Common shore crabs can be found on the beach under rocks or weeds that are well below the high-water mark. In some regions, anglers harvest crabs by laying traps that consist of sections of guttering or ridge tile that are partially buried in the mud. The crabs seek refuge in these sanctuaries as they prepare to moult and the angler can check on their progress before harvesting and storing in a cool shed or fridge prior to use. When a crab's shell starts to lift from its back, it's perfect for freezing. Crabs moult all year round in warmer climates, while in cooler climates the main moult takes place in the summer.

As well as the common shore crab there are other varieties of crabs that the angler can use as 'peelers' or soft-back bait including edible crab, the velvet swimmer, spider and hermit crabs. The hermit crab

LEFT THE OUTER SHELL IS PEELED FROM THE CRAB.

LEFT THE LEGS CAN BE PEELED TO PROVIDE SMALL BAITS.

ABOVE THE CRAB IS SECURED TO THE HOOK WITH THE HELP OF BAITING ELASTIC.

makes its home in the shells of shellfish – typically whelks – from which it can be removed and used in the same way as other crabs.

Prawns make extremely effective bait in some areas, particularly in clear water, owing to their lack of a strong scent. A prawn is best fished live on a relatively light tackle. Prawns can be collected either by using a dip net at low tide or by lowering a baited drop net beside a harbour wall.

BELOW PEELER CRAB READY FOR USE.

ABOVE PEELER CRAB CAN BE FOUND BENEATH SEAWEED.

ABOVE CRABS CAN BE HARVESTED BY USING TRAPS CONSISTING OF GUTTERING OR RIDGE TILES.

BELOW BAIT COLLECTING CAN BE HARD WORK.

BELOW A HOOK-SHAPED TOOL CAN BE USED TO REDUCE BACK STRAIN WHEN SEARCHING FOR CRABS.

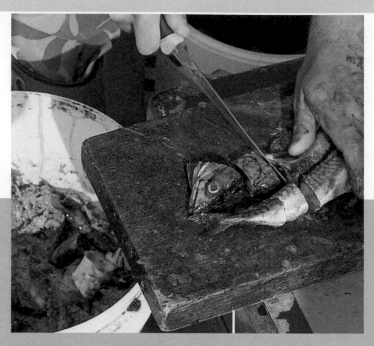

ABOVE CUTTING UP FISH FOR THE RUBBY DUBBY.

GROUNDBAIT

Although groundbait is not used as much in sea angling as it is in freshwater fishing (see page 75), it can nevertheless, be extremely effective in some situations and will draw the fish from a wide area if it is introduced carefully.

The most commonly used saltwater groundbait is 'rubby-dubby' or 'chervey', which consists of ground-up fish, fish oils and bran. 'Chum', an essential element of shark and tuna fishing, is made of larger pieces of fish and live baitfish. The rather evil smelling mix is contained in a net bag (like an onion sack) and tied to the side of the boat, where bits break off and drift in the tide, providing a tempting scent trail that stretches out behind the boat. Using its keen sense of smell, a shark will follow this 'floating buffet' and home in on the main source to find a juicy bait suspended in mid water. Similar mixtures can be used for shore fishing: an onion sack containing bread, or a rubby-dubby mix (tinned cat food mixed with bread) makes for an excellent saltwater groundbait, suspended from a harbour wall, and will attract many species, including grey mullet.

ABOVE TENSE MOMENTS AS THE ANGLER DECIDES WHEN TO SET
THE HOOK.

The further you can cast, the more sea you will be able to cover: the most basic cast is the overhead 'thump' – a style that most novices use before refining their technique. The 'off-the-ground' cast begins from a standing start with the lead on the ground: the angler leans backwards and sweeps the rod at a slight angle rather than overhead. This is used in cramped conditions for safety, such as on a crowded pier.

PENDULUM CASTING

The pendulum cast is the casting technique used by most anglers to achieve distance: the lead is swung like a pendulum to generate power and compression in the rod tip prior to the final casting stroke. It's a tricky technique to master, but can be learned, so it's worthwhile taking a few lessons. The drop is adjusted to about 1.82m (6ft) to give a steady, pendulum swing that is easy to time and control. The action begins by pushing outwards with the right hand so the sinker swings away from you, rising to

about eye level. Next, without moving your right hand, you push down on the rod handle with your left hand: the push is transferred to the rod tip, and then to the leader, so that the sinker swings past in a reverse pendulum arc that carries it past the rod and your right shoulder. As it rises to its maximum height, the leader loses some of its tension – it feels as if the sinker has disappeared. In fact it's hovering in mid-air and that moment is the signal to begin the next step of the cast. The angler turns his head to look into the air towards the target, the right hand pulls the rod forward in a 'spear-throwing' manner and the arms and hands then finish the cast with a pinch-pull action.

Both fixed-spool and multiplier reels are suited to pendulum casting but, for the first, a rod with a slightly stiff tip and plenty of flexibility in the central zone is needed. With a multiplier reel, a flexible tip rod with a fast mid-zone performs well.

FLOAT FISHING

At sea, the depth of the water and strong tides make float fishing difficult and many anglers prefer to leger with the bait fished on the sea bed instead. Float fishing can, however, be the ideal technique inside a quiet harbour or marina. A sliding float rig is essential so that the fishing depth can be adjusted continuously. Sea-angling floats are usually quite large and brightly coloured, as they need to be cast long distances and to be seen by the angler in swells, but in sheltered spots the float size can be reduced: inside a harbour a waggler can be perfect (see page 60). Alternatively, a clear bubble float can be used, where the lead is water inside the float. When float fishing, it's important to remember that the fish are more likely to spot the bait above them, silhouetted against the surface of the water, than in a murky or weedy background close to the sea bed, so nicely smelly bait will improve the chances of the fish finding the bait.

BELOW SEA-ANGLING FLOATS.

SPINNING

Many sea fish species are quite happy to chase after a lure that looks like, or mimics, the behaviour of the smaller fish and marine wildlife they live on. Lures come in a huge range of designs from a simple feather lashed to a hook to floating plugs. You can get flashing spinners, rubber eels, plastic muppets, jelly worms and giant metal pirks on treble hooks, all of which are designed to fool the fish into believing that the lure is a live fish. Shore-based anglers have to cast their lures into deep water, so need to choose an appropriate weight to gain maximum distance, but without compromising the lure's ability to mimic the action of the real fish it's replacing. Boat anglers troll a lure at a distance behind the boat so the wake and the propeller's action in the water cause water disturbance that helps to attract bigger fish, who mistake the disturbance for thrashing of a fish in distress. Just as the boat angler is moving, the shore angler who uses lures would rove up and down the beach, casting continuously into different areas.

UPTIDING AND DOWNTIDING

Boat anglers fishing into shallow waters less than 15m (50ft) deep, cast bait away from the boat, usually uptide, hence the name. This is so any noise caused by the boat's hull doesn't scare the fish. The presentation of bait hard on the sea bed in uptiding is very much like that of shore angling, and is used to target large fish like cod, bass and ray. Downtiding, as the name suggests, involves fishing with the tackle trailing downtide from an anchored boat and the baited tackle is simply lowered from the boat to the sea bed.

LEFT FISHING WITH TWO RODS (P208) DOUBLES YOUR CHANCES OF A CATCH.

BELOW THE BAITED HOOK IS DRAPED OVER THE WIRES OF THE GRIP WEIGHT BEFORE CASTING UPTIDE.

SCRATCHING

Scratching is a technique derived from competition angling, where the angler is trying to catch whatever fish are 'scratching around', fishing with a maximum of three hooks legered on the sea bed. This method keeps anglers busy and generally catches small fish, although sometimes a big specimen can take the bait too.

TWO RODS

Fishing with two rods increases the odds of catching fish, and allows the angler to target different species at the same time using different baits, different casting distances and even different fishing techniques, such as legering and float fishing. In many instances, angling clubs allow two-rod fishing but may impose a maximum use of three hooks in total, so check first.

FREELINING, TROTTING, BOOM HANGING AND BAITED SPOONS

Freelining is the use of a head-hooked ragworm or live sand eel on a freeline using light fixed-spool tackle. As the bait sinks, it 'dances' in the water, attracting fish by its movement. Trotting is fishing from the beach using a lead, which allows the baits to be drifted and trotted downtide. It can also be used for targeting flounder in river estuaries. Boom hanging is a good technique for fishing from alongside piers and harbour walls: three plastic or wire booms (spaced over 3.7m/12ft) hold the bait (small and wriggly ragworms, usually) away from the main line and keep it slightly away from the wall or stilt legs. In estuaries, many anglers may find their static baits have been gobbled up by crabs; to overcome this they cast out large metal or plastic spoons (shaped pieces with a hook attached at one end and a swivel at the other) with a hook bait positioned a few centimetres behind it. This can be retrieved slowly from the sea bed – hopefully with a flounder, plaice, pollack or coalfish having taken the bait.

The seas and oceans offer the angler a huge range of species. What you can catch depends on the waters in which you fish, and some of the most common species are outlined below.

FLATFISH AND BOTTOM FEEDERS

These species are the mainstay of sea angling in waters around the United Kingdom and provide plenty of sport when the bigger fishes are not around. As bottom-dwelling fish, flatfish prefer sand, mud and sediment sea beds on which to lie – either on their left or right side. All have both eyes facing upwards: brill and turbot are 'left eyed' while plaice, dab and sole are 'right-eyed'.

A useful set-up for catching the smaller species is to fish on three hooks on a paternoster terminal rig with hooks sized 1 or 2 and small worm baits. The best fishing times are at high water during spring tides and at dusk or dawn. The dab (*Limanda limanda*) is the smallest – and many maintain, the tastiest – of the flatfish species. The dab likes strong tides, which stir up the sea bed to release food, and many anglers find stale lugworms are attractive bait to tempt them. Dabs rarely exceed 450g (1lb) and the minimum size permitted is over 22cm (9in) long. The sole (*Solea solea*) is a nocturnal flatfish found close to the shores of sandy beaches. It has a hook-shaped mouth and likes lug- and ragworms on small hooks. The minimum size for sole is over 24cm (9½in).

RIGHT Plaice provide good sport and a delicious meal at the end of the day.

The largest flatfish caught by sea anglers around the British Isles is the halibut (*Hippoglossus hippoglossus*), which is largely fished for from boats. With its big, speckled and elongated body and large mouth, halibut can grow in excess of 90kg (200lb). Plaice (*Pleuronectes platessa*) is probably the most popular flatfish for sea anglers, who can either leger at long range from the shore or fish with light tackle from an anchored boat. Living for up to 30 years, a plaice is identifiable by its bright orange or red spots, a bony head and a white underside marked with a pattern of chevrons.

Turbot (*Scophthalmus maximus*) and brill (*Scophthalmus rhombus*) both have a large round body and a 'freckled' appearance, which can make them difficult to tell apart. Look for the frilly edge to the front of the dorsal fin, close to the mouth of the brill. Both species are common in British waters and like offshore sandbanks, but they can also be found in estuaries. Because both have large mouths, anglers use mackerel strips and sand eels for effective bait for these fish-eaters.

Whiting, (*Merlangius merlangus*), which is a bottom-feeding fish, is common around British shores from September onwards and is frequently found close to the shore after dark. It's a greedy feeder and likes lugworms, squid and fish baits and has a number of small, very sharp teeth, so watch your fingers! Shore-

LEFT SPURDOG ARE MEMBERS OF THE SHARK FAMILY.

caught whiting are rarely in excess of 900g (2lb) in weight, but the minimum permitted size is over 27cm (10½in).

A word of caution is needed here: sometimes mistaken for a small whiting is the lesser weever (*Echiichthys vipera*): this is one of the few fish with a poisonous sting to be found in British waters (see also stingray, page 216). The lesser weever grows to only a few centimetres long and is often caught from sandy, shallow beaches. Its venom is extremely painful, but can be alleviated with heat treatment. Nevertheless, in severe cases, hospitalisation is necessary.

BALLAN WRASSE
(*LABRUS BERGYLTA*)

The ballan wrasse is the largest of the five species of wrasse found in British waters – in some regions it goes by the nickname of 'rock tench'. Because it likes clear water, the wrasse is not found around estuaries, but at rocky and weedy coastal sites and around piers, where they thrive on a diet of crustacea. The adult wrasse, which can live for up to 25 years, is brightly coloured orange or red (immature fish are green with blue markings) and has large lips, a pointed snout and teeth. The ballan wrasse is remarkable for its life cycle: all fish are born female and take six years to mature. After spawning, a proportion of the fish change sex to become male. Furthermore, the wrasse is one of the few species of fish that go to 'sleep' after dark: they wedge themselves into a crevice at night to sleep.

BASS
(*DICENTRARCHUS LABRAX*)

With its silver scales and dark back, streamlined body, spiked dorsal fin and powerful forked tail, bass is considered by many sea anglers to be the prize fish – but beware the sharp edges to their gills! Bass has a liking for hugging the shoreline, so is a great fish for beginners with limited casting skills. At night, bass can often be seen cruising just a few metres below the water under harbour lights. The bass is a shoal fish, although larger members are said to be solitary. It is also a very territorial fish, regularly patrolling a specific route. Small bass can be caught on lures spun near the surface of the water and close-range live or dead baiting works for large, shore-caught bass.

COALFISH
(*POLLACHIUS VIRENS*)

Related to the pollack (see page 215), and often found alongside each other, both have large eyes, tiny scales and a big mouth with a protruding bottom lip. The coalfish is, however, a much darker bottle green colour with a straight white lateral line and forked tail. Large coalfish like to hang around deep-water wrecks, while smaller ones prefer river estuaries and harbours. The coalfish readily takes a lure and large fish bait (such as mackerel) fished from close range from the shore after winter storms. The coalfish is a fighter, so be prepared for its incredible strength and stamina.

COD (*GADUS MORHUA*)

With its green flanks, large head, belly and fins and a barbel on its lower lip, the cod is probably the most popular sea fish pursued by anglers in boats and from the shore. As a major food source, it is subject to large-scale commercial fishing, which has lead to a reduction in the average size of the fish. Cod has been known to live for up to 24 years and, while widespread in British waters, tends to prefer mixed sea beds when young, but kelp weed, reefs and wrecks when older. This fish has a bright red 'tan' from the kelp seaweed in which it lives, while in other places it is more a creamy grey-green colour. Its huge mouth betrays it as a hungry fish and it will eat a range of worms, shrimps and crab when young; when older, it prefers other fish. Shore anglers fish for cod during autumn and winter (it can be caught from boats all year round) particular, on night spring tides. Most often caught is codling, or cod that is under 2.27kg (5lb) using a tasty 'cocktail' bait of lugworm and squid that has been fished into deep water from a beach or pier.

GARFISH (*BELONE BELONE*)

With its long, eel-like body and beak, the garfish is Britain's 'mini-marlin', and an unmistakable summer species of fish in southern British waters, where it can be spotted leaping over flotsam on the surface of the water. Note that its scales come off easily and, if you are going to eat it, be prepared for green-coloured bones! The garfish is attracted to the swim by a groundbait of boiled mackerel and bread, which will put an irresistible oily slick on the surface of the water. As bait it will take sand eels and small ragworms as well as strips of fish (including their own kind).

MACKEREL (*SCOMBER SCOMBUS*)

A member of the tuna family, the mackerel is a surface-feeding fish. It likes clear water and the presence of a shoal is often betrayed by a watchful group of seagulls overhead, which circle and dive into the shoal as they chase after fry inshore. Blue-green in colour, with zebra-like markings, the mackerel has widely spaced dorsal fins and small 'finlets' near its tail. Small bait-sized mackerel are known as 'joeys'. Mackerel can be fished from a dinghy on fly-fishing tackle using a larger trout fly or using fish-strip bait, but they will even grab at an empty hook. It's worth approaching a shoal of mackerel cautiously: below the mackerel shoal may well be a shoal of bass, who can be tempted with a free-lined live mackerel or lure.

MULLET

There are three species of mullet to be found in British waters: the thick-lipped grey mullet (*Chelon labrusos*), the thin-lipped grey mullet (*Liza ramada*) and the golden grey mullet (*Liza aurata*). Known colloquially as 'grey ghosts', the mullet will glide around harbours but disappear immediately a sound or shadow is apparent. Of the three, it is the thick-lipped grey that is the major species targeted with rod and line in river estuaries, and from harbours and marinas, where it enjoys brackish water and can travel freely between salt- and freshwater. It has a grinding gizzard – ideally suited to a rough diet of mud-covered detritus – and really long intestines with which to digest it. If you want to catch a mullet, look for a sewer outfall! With its torpedo-shaped, striped, scaled body with broad head and large heart-shaped lips, the biggest fish are to be found in land-locked lagoons, where they can be attracted by a groundbait mix of bread and boiled fish and caught using a light tackle with a float or leger and a bait of bread and fish. The thin-lipped grey is a smaller fish, commonly caught on light tackle from rivers and beaches, using small ragworm fished high in the water. It comes quite far inshore to feed on maggots that can be found in rotting seaweed washed inshore by a large swell. Less often targeted, the golden grey has a slimmer body andis identifiable by its golden cheek patches. It is found in river estuaries.

POLLACK (*POLLACHIUS POLLACHIUS*)

While similar to the coalfish (see above) in both behaviour and looks, the pollack can be distinguished from its 'cousin' by a curved lateral line behind the gill covers and straight tail end. It is also a very powerful fish, but lacks the stamina of the coalfish. An effective method is to fish close to kelp, above a reef or wreck, using different coloured lures (although black is favoured by boat anglers and brighter colours preferred by shore anglers) on a long trace.

LEFT THIS FINE BLONDE RAY USED ITS WINGS TO GIVE STRONG RESISTANCE IN THE TIDE.

SKATE AND RAY

There is no biological difference between skate and ray: the word 'skate' is used to describe the bigger members of the Rajidae family, which have long snouts and include the giant common skate that can be found off the Scottish and Irish coasts. The smaller members of the family are called ray, and the three most common species in British waters are the thornback ray (*Raja clavata*), the blonde ray (*Raja brachyura*) and the stingray (*Dasyatis pastinaca*). The thornback ray is the most common ray found in UK waters and is responsible for the 'mermaids' purses' – their egg cases – that can sometimes be found along the shore line. The diamond-shaped body, covered in sharp bony thorns (on the underside too), varies in colour from grey to brown with dark spots depending on the 'qualities' of the muddy, sandy or gravely sea beds the ray inhabits. In spring it can be found inshore, and is targeted by uptiding. It can also be fished from the shore at dawn or dusk, when it comes in with the tide. The blonde ray is quite beautiful: light brown in colour, with a few cream-coloured blotches and a dense scattering of spots that spread to the wing tips, and a white underside. Rarely, if ever, caught from the shore, the blonde ray inhabits the deep-water edges of offshore sandbanks, when legering using a braid line (to combat the deep water) and a bait of whole squid or mackerel fillets. Black- to olive-coloured, with a creamy underside, the stingray has a poisonous sting in its tail: many of the largest specimens have had their stingers (or even their tails) cut off before being returned to the water – and stingrays are always returned to the water. Increasingly, because of their rarity and because they are often hooked by anglers fishing for other species, the other rays are also retuned to the water. Stingray or not, anglers do need to beware all of the rays: although they don't have sharp teeth, they do have incredibly strong jaws designed for crushing prey.

RIGHT PORBEAGLE SHARK.

SHARK

Several of the large species of 'man-eater' sharks, such thresher, porbeagle, mako and blue shark (see left) can be found in British waters. These are fished for by specialist anglers and are subject to strict conservation regulations, whereby caught specimens are tagged for monitoring and returned to the water. Two small species, the tope (*Galeorhinus galeus*) and the smoothhound (*Mustelus mustelus* and *Mustelus asterias*) are for popular fishing but note though that 'catch-and-release' is the accepted practice for all shark fishing in Britain. The tope is the biggest of the summer species in British waters, but is rarely caught from the shore. This has a 'true' shark shape and colour: slim with sharply pointed snout and large pectoral fins. The tope has one large and one small dorsal fin and sharp, triangular teeth. It lives close to a clear sea bed and rises to the top when feeding. Large, legered fish baits such as mackerel fillets on wire traces are used in both downtide and uptide boat fishing. Large specimens are difficult to land and are generally hauled out of the water by their tails: this can cause damage to the tope's stomach so it is preferable to unhook and release them while they are still in the water.

The smoothhound was called ironically called 'Sweet William' in the Middle Ages: when dead they give off a strong smell of ammonia. The two species are the 'common' and the 'starry'. The starry smooth-hound is 'ovoviviparous' – it produces its young by hatching them within their bodies, and the young are nourished by the egg sacs. The common smoothhound on the other hand is 'viviparous' – the young are born alive and are nourished directly from their mother. Both smoothhounds are relatives of the ray (see page 216) and, like it, have blunt, flat and crushing teeth (making wire traces unnecessary). They are distinguished from the tope by having two dorsal fins of equal size. The smoothhound feeds in packs and can be found in many estuary regions like the Solent, Bristol Channel and the Thames where boat anglers favour uptiding using peeler crab baits.

RIGHT STARRY SMOOTHHOUND SHARK.

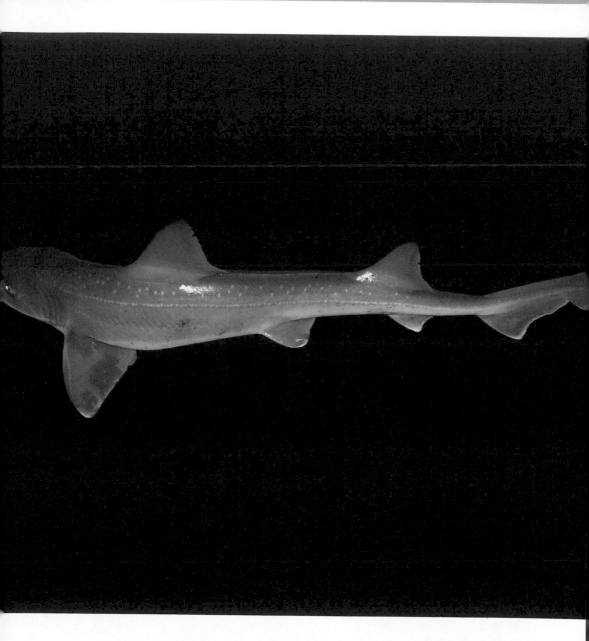

INDEX